MILITARY SOCIAL WORK PRACTICE

MILITARY SOCIAL WORK PRACTICE

Starting the Conversation

Susan Denise Barnes

Surrogate Press®

Copyright © 2023 Susan Denise Barnes
All rights reserved.

No part of this publication may be reproduced, stored in a retrieval system, or transmitted in any form or by any means, electronic, mechanical, photocopying, recording, or otherwise, without written permission of the author.

Published in the United States by
Surrogate Press®
an imprint of Faceted Press®
Surrogate Press, LLC
Park City, Utah
SurrogatePress.com

ISBN: 978-1-947459-81-6
Library of Congress Control Number: 2023907743

Book design by: Katie Mullaly, Surrogate Press®

John McCrae was a Canadian brigade surgeon who, after tending to the wounded during the 1915 Second Battle of Ypres Belgium, penned the poem, "In Flanders Fields." The first verse reads:

> "In Flanders fields the poppies blow
> Between the crosses, row on row,
> That mark our place, and in the sky
> The larks, still bravely singing, fly
> Scarce heard amid the guns below…"

Two women an ocean apart—an American named Moina Michael and a Frenchwoman named Anna Guérin—sparked a movement to honor veterans by wearing red poppies. Red poppies are worn on Memorial Day and Armistice/Veterans Day in the United States and Remembrance/Armistice Day in other countries to honor military service members who paid the ultimate sacrifice.

This book is dedicated to all current service members, veterans, and military families, and to the professionals and caring community members who help us slow down the dance with our dragons and heal mind, body, and spirit.

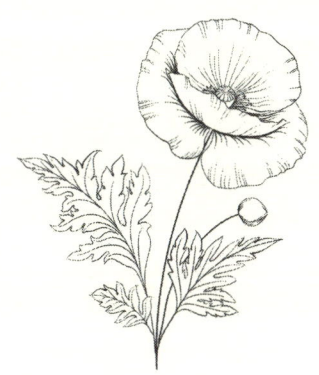

Table of Contents

Introduction 1

Chapter One: Military Cultural Competency 4

Chapter Two: The Military Institution and Culture 11

Chapter Three: Military Life 30

Chapter Four: Effect of Deployments
and Battle on Service Members 47

Chapter Five: Physical Injuries 58

Chapter Six: Invisible Wounds 71

Chapter Seven: Moral Injury 84

Chapter Eight: Family Stress and Resilience 94

Chapter Nine: The Emotional Cycle of Deployment 117

Chapter Ten: Community Capacity vis-à-vis Military,
Veteran, and Family Support Programs 134

About the Author 147

Introduction

Since the dawn of time humans have engaged in conflict and battle. Strategies, tactics, and rules of engagement have changed across time and cultures; how individuals cope with the fallout of battle has changed as well, albeit not as quickly. The care and repair of the mind, body, and spirit after battle was left to the warrior, the families, and depending on the culture, the community. Families and communities welcomed home their service members with fanfare and celebration; however, not all returned with mind, body, and spirit intact. And the country was beginning to recognize the high cost of war.

Up until World War I, not much was done in the way of mental health treatment. Medical personnel and chaplains were the only available service providers for military members. During World Wars I and II, psychiatrists were employed in both the initial screening process for recruits and for treating conditions such as shell shock. Most service members and veterans suffering from what would later be termed post-traumatic stress disorder (PTSD) were treated behind the lines or in mental/VA hospitals. Major changes would not occur until the Vietnam War.

Through the efforts of Chaim Shatan and Robert J. Lifton and the lobbying efforts of Vietnam veterans, the diagnostic designation, PTSD, was adopted and included in the 3rd edition of the *American Psychiatric Association's Diagnostic and Statistical Manual of Mental Disorders* in 1980. Having a label for the condition that haunted thousands did not automatically mean help was available. It would take time and effort to gradually erode the stigma of seeking help. Moreover, the concept of PTSD was controversial; the definition, diagnostic criteria, and treatment were all up for debate. Some even believed it was a ploy to ensure veterans got some VA benefits for their war service (Erwin, 2019; Pols & Oak, 2007). The first Gulf War and the conflicts in Iraq and Afghanistan have pushed the mental health crisis and challenges of our nation's warriors to the forefront and garnered nationwide attention.

The seminal work of Terri Tanielian and Lisa Jaycox, *Invisible Wounds of War: Psychological and Cognitive Injuries, Their Consequences, and Services to Assist Recovery*, published by the RAND Corporation, provided a catalyst for the Department of Defense and the Veterans Health Administration to take focused and aggressive action in addressing the mental health needs of our nation's veterans. The increased presence and placement of mental health professionals within military and community organizations and the explosion of family support programs across the nation reflect the efforts of those who are committed to the restoration of veterans' minds, bodies, and spirits.

Producing a current manuscript of military social work issues is challenging. The research, writing, editing, and publishing process often results in a publication that may or may not contain current material. Add to that the fact that military life and the issues it presents are fluid and ever changing. For these reasons, the character of this book is different. This book serves as a primer and a catalyst for thought and individual exploration into the military experience and the practice of mental health service delivery to military members, veterans, and their families. The presentation of material is conversational in nature and strives to point the reader toward topics for further research. This book provides the reader with a general introduction to military culture, the challenges of everyday life, consequences of deployment and battle for the service member and family, the most common battle injuries, and various support programs offered through the Department of Defense, military service branches, the Veterans Administration, and community organizations. A brief exploration of roles and settings for the military social worker is also

Introduction

presented. Hopefully, you will be inspired by these initial conversations to further research issues pertaining to military life. It is only through the collaborative efforts of professionals, volunteers, and military, government, and community organizations that we can grow our community capacity to adequately respond to the needs of military members, veterans, and their families and help them both thrive and heal mind, body, and spirit. Although the book is geared toward the social work student and professional, anyone serving or helping the military community can benefit from it.

Military Cultural Competency
CHAPTER ONE

Cultural competency is addressed in most social work courses, so presented in this chapter is a brief overview of the importance of cultural competency in social work practice followed by elements of military culture that will hopefully enhance your cultural competency in this field. Why is cultural competency important?

Typically, members of a cultural group hold the same world view; the military community is no different. Assimilation into the military culture is a key ingredient in the success of the military mission. However, the military community is a microcosm of American society. It is composed of people from many cultures and many countries. This unique feature poses challenges for leadership and supervision as well as for professionals providing military community members medical, mental health, and social services. For social workers, cultural competence is critical. First, understanding the culture of those we serve facilitates the development of a therapeutic relationship. Second, a client's culture forms the worldview and framework within which that person interprets and responds to the world. Third, when social workers are cognizant of their own cultural perspective and biases and reserve judgement when understanding clients' cultural perspective, they can develop appropriate, relevant strategies for care that reflect the client's cultural perspective. The importance of cultural competency is reflected in several professional social work documents.

Three National Association of Social Work (NASW) documents guide the conversation about the importance of cultural competency: a) *Code of Ethics of the NASW*, b), *NASW Standards and Indicators for Cultural Competence in Social Work Practice*, and c) *NASW Standards for Social Work Practice with Service Members, Veterans, and their Families*.

Our NASW Guidelines

The Preamble to the *Code of Ethics of the NASW* notes that the primary goal of social workers is to promote social justice and social change. A key element to successfully doing this is developing cultural competency regarding the racial, ethnic, religious, and gender diversity of the community within which they work. Cultural competency allows us to embody and display the NASW core values in our social work practice by responding in a culturally sensitive manner and providing culturally relevant services. Cultural competency is a key element in the charge for social workers to influence social policy and action by promoting policies that respect the cultural differences of our nation's peoples. Cultural competence is such an important element, that the NASW saw fit to publish an additional document, *NASW Standards and Indicators for Cultural Competence in Social Work Practice*.

The *NASW Standards and Indicators for Cultural Competence in Social Work Practice* document explains the importance of cultural competency in social work practice and lays out guidelines for achieving cultural competence through the identification of 10 standards/indicators. Effective social work service delivery hinges on understanding ourselves, our clientele, and the intersection of these two with the environment in which they reside. Only by understanding these elements can we formulate applicable and appropriate intervention strategies.

The path to cultural competence is multi-pronged and a continuous process. First, it involves a path of self-reflection, self-awareness, and individual efforts toward self-growth. Second, it involves a path focused on the manner in which we conduct ourselves, utilize our skills, deliver our services, and work with other professionals to empower others. Finally, it involves a path for leaders and educators to teach, train, mentor, and develop the workforce by instilling social work ethics and cultural competency. These paths form the foundation for expanding our cultural competency to encompass work with specific populations such as social work practice with the military. The NASW addresses the unique needs of the military population in the third document, *NASW Standards for Social Work Practice with Service Members, Veterans, and their Families*.

The *NASW Standards for Social Work Practice with Service Members, Veterans, and their Families* highlights the need for well-informed, culturally sensitive, and competent practitioners to meet the ever-growing needs of the military community. The aftermath of prolonged military conflicts results in long-term challenges and effects experienced by service members and families. It is the responsibility of the social worker to become knowledgeable in military culture, the issues the military community members face, resources and institutions available to address service-related conditions, and understand evidence-based treatments and interventions. This book focuses on Standard/Indicator 8, Professional Education, and provides a foundation for understanding the military culture and need for practitioners schooled in this specialization. The Council on Social Work Education (CSWE) recognized the importance of military social work as an educational and professional specialization, thus publishing the 2010 document *Advanced Social Work Practice in Military Social Work*. Noting the involvement and training of mental health workers since 1918, the CSWE argues that the need for social workers is more critical than ever given the longest sustained combat situations that our armed forces have been engaged in since Operation Desert Storm, 16 January 1991. This recognition led to the development of the 2015 *Specialized Practice Curricular Guide for Military Social Work*. Furthermore, Wooten's 2015 article, *Military Social Work: Opportunities and Challenges for Social Work Education*, presents the argument for the need for a military social work specialization grounded in knowledge of the military culture and evidence-based practices to assist the military members, veterans, and family members in their healing journey. Wooten's arguments are based on NASW and CSWE leaders' identification of the need for specialized education and training and the publication of guidelines to foster this specialized education and training. Finally, Wooten highlights the requisite knowledge, skills, and abilities (KSA) for a social worker at the micro, mezzo, and macro levels of practice. With an understanding of the importance of military social workers, some settings and roles a social worker might perform are highlighted in the next section.

Military Social Work Settings and Roles

The case has been made that there is a strong need for military social work professionals. It is a specific social work field that focuses on service to individuals and families who are part of the military community. Moreover, military social work requires a specific set of KSAs to effectively work with military members and families. These KSAs include a) cultural competence of military culture and various ethnic cultures; b) counseling and resource management skills; c) knowledge of common military issues such as those resulting from separations and battle; and d) knowledge of military health care systems. These KSAs are put into practice while providing services to the military community.

When serving military members, veterans, and their families, social workers assume many roles and work in a variety of settings. These settings and roles are as varied as in any other social work field. They include a) individual or family counselor; b) case manager, service broker, or advocate; c) policy advocate or developer; d) family, community, or university educator; e) consultant or liaison; and f) researcher. Where do social workers assume these roles? Settings in which a military social worker can practice include four primary settings: a military installation, a deployed location, a Veteran's Health Administration facility, and in the local community.

There are many places on a military installation in which a social worker can be employed. As a military member or a civilian, social workers can be employed at the mental health clinic which serves active duty members. Here social workers provide traditional counseling and therapy. The focus is on strengthening the service members' mental health so they can successfully carry out their duties. Second, recognizing the need for rapid assessment and treatment of battle injuries and trauma, social workers have been deployed and embedded in military units on the front lines along with medical personnel. A third location where social workers can be employed is at a family advocacy office which focuses on the prevention and intervention of child abuse and neglect, and domestic abuse/intimate partner violence in military families. The social worker coordinates efforts with various civilian and military social services, and medical and legal agencies to craft a coordinated plan of action. The fourth place a social worker may be employed is with the medical clinic or hospital in alcohol and drug abuse prevention and treatment program. A fifth setting in which a social worker may be found is within the DoD schools that are located on military installations around the world. Their knowledge of military life and resources available is invaluable to the success of students within those schools. Finally, family support centers (each branch of service has a different name for these centers) often employ social workers to serve as military family life counselors. In this role, they counsel family members and provide family education, resources, and support services to members and their families.

At Veterans Health Administration facilities, social workers work in VA hospitals, medical centers, and VA community clinics providing counseling, case management, discharge planning, and veteran and family education. They can also help secure housing and specialized services for the veteran and caregiver. You can find more information at socialwork.va.gov

Finally, in the local community, social workers provide resources, support, and therapeutic services to members and families in mental health and social service centers, private practice, and through their employment with not-for-profit organizations. They may provide individual or group counseling and may specialize in service-related issues such as PTSD, traumatic brain injury (TBI), substance abuse, family violence, or military sexual assault.

Some social workers work with families conducting initial assessments (mental health, biopsychosocial, strengths), counseling and therapy, providing crisis intervention, substance abuse intervention, suicide prevention and family care, family violence prevention and intervention. Of course, client education, information and referral, as well as caregiver support and case management are additional social work functions.

Providing the social worker with the necessary professional and technical skills along with a basic understanding of military culture is the basis for Standard/Indicator 8, Professional Education. Also, understanding military social work settings and roles helps guide the social worker down the desired path. Finally, to understand how social workers can effectively serve the military population, a basic understanding of the military institution and its culture is necessary.

Final Thoughts

The military is a microcosm of society and a unique culture in its own right, so competency in this field is necessary. Cultural competency is an essential ingredient of social work practice as noted in the NASW Standards of Cultural Competence in Social Work Practice. Guidance for working with military populations is outlined in the *NASW Standards for Social Work Practice with Service Members, Veterans, and their Families, NASW Standards and Indicators for Cultural Competence in Social Work Practice,* and the CSWE publications *Advanced Social Work Practice in Military Social Work* and *Specialized Practice Curricular Guide for Military Social Work.* Social workers serve the military population in a variety of settings both on and off military installations and as employees of the Veterans Health Administration. The roles they play are the same—client educators, therapists, case managers, advocates, crisis counselors, researchers, policy developers, volunteer coordinators/trainers, and educators in colleges and universities.

Although the primary audience for this book is social work practitioners, students, and instructors, anyone—professional, volunteer, service member, veteran, family member or friend—who has a connection to the military community can benefit from the information presented here.

References

Council on Social Work Education. (2010). *Advanced social work practice in military social work.*

Council on Social Work Education. (2015). *Specialized practice curricular guide for military social work.*

Erwin, S. K. (2019). American veterans and the evolutions of mental health: A historical review of diagnoses and depiction. *Journal of Veteran Studies, 4*(1), 47-57.

National Association of Social Workers. (2018). *Code of ethics of the NASW.*

National Association of Social Workers. (2015). *NASW standards and indicators for cultural competence in social work practice.*

National Association of Social Workers. (2012). *NASW standards for social work practice with service members, veterans, and their families.*

Pols, H., & Oak, S. (2007). War and military mental health: The US psychiatric response in the 20th century. *American Journal of Public Health, 97*(12), 2132-2142.

Wooten, N. R. (2015). Military social work: Opportunities and challenges for social work education. *Journal of Social Work Education. 51*(Suppl 1), S6–S25.

The Military Institution and Culture
CHAPTER TWO

Perusing sociology books and websites, there is variance in the number of institutions that exist within a society. The basic list of five institutions—family, education, religion, economy, and government—is often expanded to include community, medicine, healthcare, and others. Within the government institution lies the military. In this chapter we explore the military institution, its components, and salient features.

Elements of Institutions and Their Culture

Each institution has elements that describe the culture. The main cultural elements we find in the military include a) formal organizational structure, b) hierarchy of roles and responsibilities, c) set of shared core values, d) language and terminology, and e) traditions and customs.

Formal Organizational Structure

Every organization is structured in a way that supports and perpetuates the purpose of that organization. The military is structured in a way that maximizes order, discipline, and mission accomplishment. Additionally, there is a basic military organization that identifies enlisted and officer rank structure. Within each branch of the military (Army, Air Force, Marines, Navy, Coast Guard), there is a formal organizational structure that is dictated primarily by roles and functions of that branch.

Branches of the Military. There are six branches of the military. The Army, Air Force, Marines, Navy, and newly formed Space Force fall under the Department of Defense. The Coast Guard falls under the Department of Homeland Security. The *Department of Defense Directive 5100.01 Functions of the Department of Defense and Its Major Components* describes each branch of the military and its functions. The most current version of this directive is 2010; however, several attempts have been made to update it and incorporate changes and new departments. One of many changes was the establishment of the Department of Homeland Security and moving the Coast Guard under that department. In 2020, the Department of Defense issued the *White Paper: Evolution of Department of Defense Directive 5100.01* which explained that in "leadership changes, emerging priorities, and the proximity to a Presidential election made an 'Administrative Change' a more executable option" (DoD, 2020, p. i). The following information regarding the branches of the military are gleaned from the 2010 version of the DoDD 5100.01.

Common Military Functions. All branches of the military have a common function of providing conventional, strategic, and special operations forces to conduct operations defined by president and secretary of defense. To accomplish this, the branches a) develop concepts, doctrine, tactics, techniques, and procedures to carry out mission; b) organize, train, equip, and provide land, naval, air, space, and cyberspace forces; c) determine military service force requirements to support national security objectives; and d) monitor and assess military service operational readiness and capabilities of forces (DoD, 2010). Each military service branch has a specific function.

The US Department of the Army is the primary land force and as such it organizes, develops, and deploys land, aviation, and water transport forces for prompt and sustained combat operations on land. It is also responsible for preparing land forces necessary for effective prosecution of war and other military operations. The Army National Guard has the dual mission of protecting home states and defending the United States and its interests worldwide. Each state has its own Guard, as required by the Constitution. The Army National Guard is the only branch of the military whose existence is required by the Constitution (DoD, 2010).

The Military Institution and Culture

Operational Units of Army, from highest level of command to lowest include:
- Department of the Army
- Field Army (2-5 Corps)
- Corps (2-5 Divisions)
- Division (3 Brigades; 10,000 – 18,000 soldiers)
- Brigade (3 or more Battalions; 3000-5,000 soldiers)
- Battalion (3-5 Companies; 300-500 soldiers)
- Company (3-4 Platoons; 100-200 soldiers)
- Platoon (3-4 Squads; 16-40 soldiers)
- Squad (4-10 soldiers)

The US Department of Air Force consists of active duty and reserve units. It is the principal air and space force, providing air and space support to US military forces and joint forces to ensure air, space, and cyberspace dominance. The Air Force conducts close air support for ground forces; provides transport equipment and supplies to forward-based forces; conducts reconnaissance and air interdiction support; and provides combat control, air rescue and recovery, and intelligence support to other US and joint forces. The Air National Guard is a separate reserve component of the Air Force. Like the Army National Guard, it also has dual federal and state missions. It is responsible for air defense of the entire United States and prepares its units for prompt mobilization during war, national emergencies, natural disasters, and civil disturbances (DoD, 2010).

Operational Units of Air Force, from highest level of command to lowest include:
- Department of the Air Force
- Major Command: organized by mission stateside; region overseas
- Numbered Air Force: key role during war time
- Wing: 2 or more groups; specific mission; responsible for AF base (min. 1,000 personnel)

- Group: 2 or more squadrons with similar functions (min 400 personnel)
- Squadron: 2 or more flights; min 35 personnel
- Flight: 2 or more personnel make a flight

The newly formed US Space Force is separate branch of service that falls under the direction of the US Air Force and is responsible for organizing, training, and equipping members to conduct global space operations to enhance joint and coalition forces and identify decision-making options to achieve national objectives. The US Space Command was redesignated the US Space Force in December 2019 because of growing threats to the space arena. Securing air space is a national security imperative and the establishment of a unique branch to focus solely on space dominance and superiority was vital to achieve this objective. Air Force personnel serving in this new branch are called Guardians and wear distinctive uniforms and insignia.

The US Department of Navy also is comprised of active duty and reserve units. The Navy and Marine Corps are principal maritime forces. The Navy consists of land, surface (ships), and submarine forces. The function of the Navy is to prepare, develop, and deploy naval, land, air, space, and cyberspace forces necessary to support its own service branch and the other military services. They conduct operations to achieve and maintain sea control through subsurface, surface, land, air, space, and cyberspace dominance. Finally, the Navy is responsible for maintaining and defending sea bases in support of naval, amphibious, land, air, or other joint operations (DoD, 2010).

Operational Units of Navy from highest level of command to lowest include:
- Department of the Navy
- Combatant commands
- Component commands
- Numbered Fleets
- Task Force or Battle Fleet
- Task Group

The Military Institution and Culture

- Squadron or Task Unit
- Flotilla
- Task Element

The US Marine Corps also has active duty and reserve units. It is typically the "first in" organization and provides forces to conduct combined arms air ground task forces and to serve as an expeditionary force-in-readiness. The Marines are an advanced force responsible for the initial seizure of land and amphibious assaults to ensure access by other military services. The air component of the Marines provides close air support for land forces (DoD, 2010).

Operational Units of Marine Corps from highest level of command to lowest include:

- Division: commanded by major general; consists of 3 regiments and headquarters (HQ) battalion
- Regiment: commanded by colonel; consists of 3 battalions and a HQ battalion
- Battalion: commanded by lt. colonel; consists of 3 companies and HQ/Service company
- Company: commanded by captain or major; consists of 3 platoons and company HQ
- Platoon: commanded by 1st lieutenant and senior NCO; consists of 3 squads
- Squad: led by sergeant; consists of 3 teams
- Team: basic unit; led by corporal and consists of 4 marines

The Coast Guard was established in 1790 and is one of the oldest organizations in the federal government. It provided armed services until the Navy was established 8 years later to take over that function. The US Coast Guard used to fall under the Department of Transportation, but now falls under Department of Homeland Security and has both a peacetime and wartime mission. The peacetime mission involves activities to protect US coastal ways and seas; maintain safety and security of US waters; provide maritime homeland security and counterterrorism; conduct port operations, security, defense, and counter-illicit trafficking operations (e.g., drug interdiction); and conduct search and rescue operations. When called into national service, the Coast Guard falls under the Navy (DoD, 2010).

Even though the Coast Guard is a military organization, it falls under the Department of Homeland Security (DHS), not the Department of Defense (DoD). The 2018-2019 presidential furlough drove home this distinction. While the military branches continued to get paid, Coast Guard members did not get paid during the furlough because they fell under the DHS and not the DoD.

As mentioned earlier, service branches have military reserve components as part of their total force composition: Army National Guard, Army Reserve, Navy Reserve, Marine Corps Reserve, Air National Guard, Air Force Reserve, and Coast Guard Reserve. These reserve forces are activated in times of war or national emergency as declared by the president or Congress.

The National Guard and Reserve Forces of the US Military perform vital functions within the Department of Defense. They not only perform similar missions as their active duty counterparts, often they have unique roles as well. Each branch of the military has a Reserve component that serves to augment and complement active duty operations. Reserve units and personnel are classified as federal military units/personnel. On the other hand, the Army and Air Force are the only branches with National Guard units. National Guard units/personnel are classified as "dual enrolled;" they fall under the control of the governor of their state unless called into federal service by the president.

The National Guard performs many functions: assistance in domestic crises and disasters, combat missions overseas, working with the Coast Guard and other agencies in counterdrug operations, and helping with reconstruction efforts. National Guard members typically hold civilian jobs or attend college while serving in the National Guard.

The Military Institution and Culture

Reserve and Guard members may be categorized in one of several ways depending on their level of service. We focus on three categories here—the Active Guard and Reserve, the Select Reserve Units, and the Military Reserve Technicians.

The Active Guard and Reserve is comprised of military personnel who serve full-time as active duty members of their unit. Members filling these billets ensure the unit functions on an on-going basis while most members serve in a part-time capacity. This part-time service is referred to as selected reserve. Selected Reserve Unit members are what many refer to as "weekend warriors." Most reservists and guardsmen are classified as selected reserve members. During peacetime, members train one weekend a month (drill weekend) and again during a 2-week period. Finally, Military Reserve Technicians hold a dual status of federal employee (civil service employee) and military member. In this position, reserve technicians do not qualify for active-duty military pensions; however, they do receive federal employee and retirement benefits and qualify for reserve military pensions.

This is not the only distinction between Guard and Reserve members and traditional active duty military members/units. Since these are typically part-time careers, many members live far from their training sites. Guard members may travel across the state for their training while Reservists may travel across country to train with their unit. Many Reserve units share facilities with their active duty counterparts; however, they are not authorized to live in military housing. On the other hand, National Guard bases do not have housing and often have very limited shopping facilities for their members. Shopping outlets typically provide uniform items and quick stop shopping items. Since traveling to the training site is common, families typically remain at home. Families may lack access to military installations, military support programs, etc. For example, health care may be limited or non-existent for Guard and Reservists (Barnes, 2022).

Full service benefits do not apply until the Guard or Reserve member is activated for 30 days or more. For more information about Tricare benefits, read https://www.tricare.mil/Plans/Eligibility/NGRMandFamilies

Hierarchy of Roles and Responsibilities

Institutions have a formal organizational hierarchy with specific roles and responsibilities to ensure organizational goals are accomplished. Those at the top of the hierarchy have a broad span of control and set policy for the entire organization. Each successive level in the hierarchy has narrower scope and span of control over the lower levels. To accomplish the military mission, direction, orders, and span of control flow from the Department of Defense, to geographic and mission specific command levels, to individual branches of the military and their unique hierarchies of branch-specific levels. Each level has specific functions and responsibilities, receiving direction from and being accountable to the echelons above it. Not only is there a hierarchy of departments within each branch of the military, there also is a rank structure that makes up what is called the chain of command. Below are the officer and enlisted rank titles for each branch of service.

Officer Ranks

Rank	Army, Air Force, Marines	Navy, Coast Guard
O-10	General (4 stars)	Admiral (4 stars)
O-9	Lieutenant General (3 stars)	Vice Admiral (3 stars)
O-8	Major General (2 stars)	Rear Admiral Upper Half (2 stars)
O-7	Brigadier General (1 star)	Real Admiral Lower Half (1 star)
O-6	Colonel	Captain
O-5	Lieutenant Colonel	Commander
O-4	Major	Lieutenant Commander
O-3	Captain	Lieutenant
O-2	First Lieutenant	Lieutenant Junior Grade
O-1	Second Lieutenant	Ensign

The Military Institution and Culture

Enlisted Ranks

Rank	Army	Air Force	Marines	Navy, Coast Guard
E-9	Sergeant Major	Chief Master Sergeant	Sergeant Major	Master Chief Petty Officer
E-8	Master Sergeant	Senior Master Sergeant	Master Sergeant	Senior Chief Petty Officer
E-7	Sergeant 1st Class	Master Sergeant	Gunnery Sergeant	Chief Petty Officer
E-6	Staff Sergeant	Technical Sergeant	Staff Sergeant	Petty Officer 1st Class
E-5	Sergeant	Staff Sergeant	Sergeant	Petty Officer 2d Class
E-4	Corporal	Senior Airman	Corporal	Petty Officer 3d Class
E-3	Private 1st Class	Airman 1st Class	Lance Corporal	Seaman
E-2	Private E-2	Airman	Private First	Seaman Apprentice
E-1	Private E-1	Airman Basic	Private	Seaman Recruit

Warrant Officer Ranks. The Army, Navy, Marine Corps, and Coast Guard all have warrant officers. They are a unique breed between officer and enlisted ranks. Warrant officers are commissioned officers and provide technical expertise and leadership to members of their units. One other unique characteristic is that warrant officers are not required to have a college degree like other commissioned officers. There are four levels for warrant officers: WO1 Warrant Officer, CW2 Chief Warrant Officer 2, CW3 Chief Warrant Officer 3, and CW4 Chief Warrant Officer 4.

Inherent in the formal hierarchy of the military institution are a set of rules and the expectation for adherence to those rules. The rules and regulations set forth in the military structure require—and demand—strict discipline when executing those rules. Members in the chain of command are responsible for enforcing rules, regulations, and adherence to these rules and regulations. Additionally, formal institutions such as the military usually have a set of core values that members live by.

Set of Core Values
Values are beliefs or ideals shared by the members of a culture that guide their attitudes, behavior, and decision-making process in all situations. Each branch of the military has a set of core values.

Note the similarities.
> Air Force: integrity first, service before self, excellence in all we do
> Army: loyalty, duty, respect, selfless service, honor, integrity, personal courage
> Navy: honor, courage, commitment
> Marines: honor, courage, commitment
> Coast Guard: honor, respect, devotion to duty

Language and Terminology
Language is a system of words or symbols that a culture uses to communicate with one another. Military language includes terms such as commissary, base/post exchange (BX/PX), civvies, leave, TDY, PCS, MOS, got your six, and many others. Not only does the military as a collective entity have a unique language, but each branch of service also has its own set of terms. Moreover, as military branches become more effective through joint force operations, new acronyms are developed. As a social worker, being familiar with the basic terms will be helpful. The Department of Defense has a military terms dictionary (700 pages) you can view online at https://dcsg9.army.mil/assets/docs/dod-terms.pdf

Traditions and Customs
Traditions and customs refer to long standing practices and the specific way in which activities are executed or performed. Traditions include wearing uniforms, displaying unit guidons, and participating in ceremonies (change of command, promotion, retirement, drill/parades). Customs are the specific way in which things are done. Courtesies are acts of behavior that support

the respect members show to one another. Saluting is a type of courtesy. Sometimes customs and courtesies are spelled out in regulations; other times they are time-honored practices. Customs and courtesies serve as a foundation for discipline, order, camaraderie, and respect. They inform military members how to behave in a variety of situations. Some of the more common customs and courtesies are saluting and addressing/showing respect to other members of the military. You can find more information about military traditions and customs by conducting an internet search.

Understanding Military Culture is Important

The military culture operates on the micro, mezzo, and macro levels. On the micro level, individuals who serve in the military are embedded in and influenced by the military culture. The military culture also encompasses and influences the family life of military members on the mezzo level. Finally, when there is a strong or large military presence in a community, the military culture often has an influence on community members as well.

As social workers dealing with military members and families, it is important to understand how military culture influences people on all three levels—micro, mezzo, macro. You may work as an individual or family counselor, a program manager, or community activist. The better you understand the levels of interaction and span of influence the military culture has on individuals, families, and communities, the better you will be able to identify strategies and resources for intervention.

Helpful websites include those that pertain to the Department of Defense, and each branch of the military: Air Force, Army, Marines, Navy, and Coast Guard. You can also find information at National Guard and Reserve websites.

Diversity in the Military

Diversity considerations in social work practice are a natural extension of cultural competency. In every social work course, we learn how diversity informs our practice with various populations. Working with the military population is no different; the military culture and the culture of the specific client population become entwined and require us to think a bit more when assessing and devising a treatment plan.

The *NASW Standards for Cultural Competency* (2015) are particularly relevant to this topic of diversity. Standard 3, Cross-cultural Knowledge, emphasizes the importance of social workers understanding the unique history and elements of diverse groups' culture from all angles such as ethnic, religious, gender, disability, and other considerations. Standard 4, Cross-cultural skills, and Standard 5, Service Delivery charge the social worker with understanding how diverse backgrounds and experiences inform the skills required and services diverse groups may need to enhance their lives. Naturally, the other standards have a bearing on social work practice with the military, but these seem most salient in this discussion. The *NASW Standards for Professional Practice when Working with Military Families* (2012) further elaborates on working with members of the military community.

NASW Standard 3, Knowledge, and Standard 4, Assessment, spell out the need for social workers to obtain and use specific knowledge regarding the military experience and culture and weave it into their toolbox of relevant theories and social work practices. Furthermore, when assessing members of the military community, a key factor again is the ability to conduct a bio-psycho-social assessment based on an understanding of the military experience followed by the appropriate selection and application of evidence-based practices. These standards require a continuous-learning attitude. Cultural competency is a life-long learning practice for the social worker. We begin to understand diversity within the military with a brief discussion of challenges with integration and inclusion.

"The military" is often thought of as a microcosm of society. Not only does military life have its own culture, but it is also populated by people from various cultures from across the country. Historically, the military institution has experienced growing pains regarding acceptance and integration of diverse groups into the military. Long before integration policies came into law, marginalized groups were a part of the US military. Unfortunately, their service was limited, and often segregated, based on the prevailing attitudes and laws at the time. Each major war and conflict generated attitudes toward certain ethnic groups that resulted in formal and informal racist, discriminatory, and hate- or fear-driven actions. The marginalized members of these military units fought two battles—one against the enemy and one against racism, bigotry, and discrimination from their own units and country. Despite the discrimination and limitations, marginalized members found a way to contribute to the success of the military mission in profound ways. Below is a sampling of some of the diverse groups that have served our country. The accompanying websites provide the details. Their journey and accomplishments paved the way for the continued integration of diverse groups and more importantly, recognition of the important contributions each diverse group makes to the military mission.

Nurses of WWII, Korean and Vietnam Wars

In the early years of the military women were relegated to clerical or nursing duties. While not on the front lines, nurses especially saw the fallout of battle. Grace E. F. Holmes gathered stories from nurses who served in WWI and compiled them in a book called *North Dakota Nurses Over There 1917-1919*. This is just one of many resources that relate the contributions of women in the early wars. You can read excerpts from this 2017 online magazine article from the American Legion: https://www.legion.org/magazine/239195/%E2%80%98goodbye-and-good-luck%E2%80%99

Women Airforce Service Pilots (WASP)

When WWII broke out, the country needed planes and pilots to fly them. They also needed pilots to test new models and deliver these planes to their training grounds throughout the country. The men went to war and in 1942, 28 civilian women pilots volunteered and formed a squadron to take on the job of testing and transporting the planes to their designated bases (Holmes, 2017). By December 1944, 1,074 more women were trained to fly aircraft.

While the men were being trained to fly one type of aircraft for war, the women air service pilots (WASP) were required to learn how to fly as many as 8 different aircraft so they could be delivered to training units across the country. Not only did they deliver the aircraft and personnel, but they were also instrumental in testing new designs and conducting flight checks after inspections and modifications. Despite General Hap Arnold's efforts to make the WASP an official part of the Air Force, the request was denied. It was not until 1977 that the WASP were recognized and granted military status. You can visit their museum in Stillwater, Texas and read more about them at this website: https://waspmuseum.org/

The 6888th Central Postal Directory Battalion of WW II

Other contributions by women in the early years are found in the history of the 6888th Central Postal Directory Battalion of WWII. This Army unit was the only all-African American, all-female unit deployed overseas during World War II (The Women of the 6888th Central Postal Directory Battalion website [https://www.womenofthe6888th.org/] notes that the unit was multi-ethnic, with members from Latino/Hispanic backgrounds that were classified as "Black" during this period). The battalion and its four companies were responsible for military mail service operation in Europe. Based in England, they were initially charged with sorting and delivering mail that had sat in warehouses for 2 years, then developing a system to keep mail moving (Hymel, 2023). You can learn more about this unit at this site: https://armyhistory.org/6888th-central-postal-directory-battalion/

Tuskegee Airmen

Up until 1948 when President Truman signed an executive order desegregating the military, African American and Asian-American service members served in separate units. Despite bigotry and racism by other military members, the Tuskegee Airmen were some of the most successful fighter pilots in WWII. The men came from all parts of the country, with varying educational backgrounds to form Army Air Corp flying squadrons and ground support

units. They were pilots, bombardiers, gunners, mechanics, air traffic controllers, clerks, police, and the various support personnel that make up a military unit. Nine hundred ninety-two (992) pilots graduated between 1942 and 1946 and the units in which they served flew throughout the European Theater of Operations. Perhaps the most well-known of the Tuskegee Airmen are the members of the 332nd Fighter Group, nicknamed the "Red Tails." You can visit their museums in Tuskegee, Alabama (now part of the national parks system)and Detroit, Michigan or read about their accomplishments at these websites: https://www.tuskegeemuseum.org
https://www.nps.gov/museum/exhibits/tuskegee_airmen/index.html

Navajo Code Talkers

The Navajo Code Talker program was the idea of Phillip Johnston, son of a missionary who grew up on a Navajo Reservation. Aware of the success of Indian code talkers during World War I, Johnston approached the Marines and suggested the use of the Navajo language to build a secret code (Paul, 1973). The program began with 29 recruits who created the original code using single words to denote phrases rather than translating word for word, thus speeding up the delivery of messages and confusing the enemy. According to the national archives there were 375-420 Code Talkers by the war's end and the program remained classified until 1968 (Jevic, 2001). Code Talkers were embedded in Marine units and were involved in every major Marine operation in the Pacific theater. The Navajo Code was never broken (Office of the Director of National Intelligence, 2023). More information can be found at:

https://www.nationalww2museum.org/war/articles/american-indian-code-talkers

https://www.intelligence.gov/people/barrier-breakers-in-history/453-navajo-code-talkers

https://www.archives.gov/publications/prologue/2001/winter/navajo-code-talkers.html

Asian-Pacific American Service Members

Asian-Pacific Americans have served with distinction in the miliary since the Civil War. They too served in segregated units because of their race. Despite racism, especially during WWII, many Nisei (American born sons of Japanese immigrants) enlisted in the military. Soldiers served in Europe, North Africa and in the Pacific theater. Units of note include the 442nd Regimental Combat Team, the 100th Infantry Battalion, and the U.S. Army's Philippine Scouts during WWII and the Korean Augmentation to the U.S. Army (KATUSA). Details of these units and many individuals can be found at https://www.army.mil/asianpacificamericans/timeline.html#unithistories and https://www.army.mil/asianpacificamericans/profiles.html

Latino/Hispanic American Service Members

The Latino and Hispanic communities have also served with distinction since the Civil War while battling for equality and against discrimination. Although American born, many are perceived as illegal immigrants by the general population. Both men and women see miliary service as a way to advance their assimilation into mainstream society and improve their economic status (Opreza, n.d.).

Honor and Fidelity: The 65th Infantry in Korea, 1950-1953, written by Gilberto N. Villahermosa chronicles the accomplishments of an all-Puerto Rican unit deployed to Korea. The unit was formed at the beginning of the 19th century to protect American interests in the Caribbean. Members of the unit fought in WWI, WWII, and Korea before being deactivated and transferred to the Puerto Rican National Guard. The book can be downloaded for free from https://www.history.army.mil/html/books/korea/65Inf_Korea/index.html

LGTB+ Service Members

The groups described above faced segregation and discrimination based on historical and prevailing prejudices and policies. For the LGB community, specific policy was developed during WW II to exclude gay individuals from serving in the military. The Selective Service sought out the assistance of three psychiatrists to develop screening tools to identify homosexuals [*term used at the time*] and prevent them from joining the military. Once again, the argument was that unit cohesion, morale, and mission accomplishment could be jeopardized. If service members were found to be gay, through act or self-disclosure, they could be dishonorably discharged (Berube, 1990). The Clinton administration created the Don't Ask, Don't Tell policy in 1993 under the DoD Directive 1304.26 (Section E1.2.8. Provisions Related to Homosexual Conduct) to allow gay personnel to serve; however, this policy create unforeseen consequences. The policy stipulated that non-heterosexual individuals could serve in the military; however, they could not reveal their sexual orientation. Service members found themselves living secret lives, were subject to harassment that they could not report lest they revealed their sexual orientation and were not eligible for benefits given to others in relationships. Co-workers, supervisors, commanders, and medical and mental health personnel were also in a difficult situation, since they were required to report and take action against those who violated anti-homosexual policy. Almost 20 years later, in 2011, the DADT policy was repealed. This was a major milestone; however, there was still work to be done. The Defense of Marriage Act (DOMA) signed by President Bill Clinton in 1996 prevented same-sex couples from receiving benefits available to other married couples under federal law, despite being eligible in for benefits in their home states. Section 3 of the DOMA was overturned in 2013 by the Supreme Court. Finally, in 2021, the DoD released new policy for transgender persons to serve in the military.

There are several sources that highlight LGBT military service. Alan Berube's book, *Coming Out Under Fire: The History of Gay Men And Women in World War II* (Twentieth Anniversary Edition) gives a great account of how anti-gay policy came about in the military and details the experiences of men and women who served during WWII. This National WWII Museum website contains a recap of a 1994 documentary based on Berube's book. https://www.nationalww2museum.org/war/articles/gay-and-lesbian-service-members

Steve Estes' book *Ask and Tell* contains 50+ interviews that chronicle the experiences of LGB service members over a span of 65 years. A book covering more recent wars that may be of interest is *Conduct Unbecoming: Lesbians and Gays in the U.S. Military: Vietnam to the Persian Gulf* by Randy Shilts.

These examples and resources for each group highlight some of the accomplishments they achieved in an environment that was not always welcoming. It is important to understand the ongoing struggles for equity for diverse populations from an historical context when serving military community members.

Cultural competency is vital to effective social work practice. This is true when working with military members and families. This competency can be further developed with an understanding of the military way of life—why people join the military, why they stay, and the challenges they and their families face during and after military service. We investigate these particulars in the next chapter.

Final Thoughts

The military has its own institutional elements and its own culture. Elements include a) formal organizational structure, b) hierarchy of roles and responsibilities, c) set of shared core values, d) language and terminology, and e) traditions and customs. Understanding military culture is important if social workers wish to be effective in providing services to military personnel, veterans, and families. Cultural competency regarding diverse groups is another essential layer of consideration when working with the military population. Diversity exists within the military just as it does in the broader population. The road to inclusion and appreciating what diversity adds to the military mission and success has not been an easy one. Readers can learn about changes in policies and laws regarding diversity in the military by subscribing to various military organizations' newsletters (VA, military.com, veterans' organizations, etc.).

References

Asian Americans and Pacific Islanders in US Army. (2023). https://www.army.mil/asianpacificamericans/timeline.html#unithistories

Barnes, S. D. (2022). *Service in the coast guard, national guard, and reserve components* [Module overview]. Canvas. https://wnmu.instructure.com/login/canvas

Berube, A. (1990) *Coming out under fire: The history of gay men and women in World War II* (Twentieth Anniversary Edition). University of North Carolina Press.

Department of Defense (DoD). (2010). *DoD Directive 5100.01 Functions of the department of defense and its major components.*

Department of Defense (DoD). (2020). *White paper: Evolution of department of defense directive 5100.01 functions of the department of defense and its major components.*

Holmes, G. E. F (2017, September 20). Good-bye and good luck. *American Legion Magazine.* https://www.legion.org/magazine/239195/%E2%80%98goodbye-and-good-luck%E2%80%99

Hymel, K.M. (2023). *The 6668th Central Postal Directory Battalion.* National Museum of the US Army. Retrieved 9 January 2023 from https://armyhistory.org/6888th-central-postal-directory-battalion/

Jevik, A. (2001). Semper fidelis, code talkers. *Prologue Magazine, 33* (4). https://www.archives.gov/publications/prologue/2001/winter/navajo-code-talkers.html

Office of the Director of National Intelligence. (2023). *1942: Navajo code talkers: Inventors of the unbreakable code.* Retrieved 9 January 2023 from https://www.intelligence.gov/people/barrier-breakers-in-history/453-navajo-code-talkers

Opreza, L. (n.d.) American Latino theme study: Military. National Park Service. Retrieved 9 January 2023 from https://www.nps.gov/articles/latinothememilitary.htm

Paul, D. A. (1973). *The Navajo Code Talkers.* Dorrance Publishing.

Villahermosa, G. N. (2009). *Honor and fidelity: The 65th infantry in Korea, 1950-1953.* Center of Military History, United States Army. https://www.history.army.mil/html/books/korea/65Inf_Korea/65Inf_KW.pdf

Military Life
CHAPTER THREE

The journey through military life starts with the decision to enter the military and ends with life after military service as a veteran. While the journey contains milestones similar to civilian life, there are many elements unique to the military culture. The military is a community with all that entails—people with common experiences and work that bind them together, institutions, organizations, and support systems that sustain and foster community stability, etc. Military life reflects core values of the military institution, so there are hints of groupthink and shared worldviews. Furthermore, due to the mobile nature of military service, service members and their families experience frequent moves and separations. Many careers in the civilian sector require moves and separations; however, the frequency with which military members and families move is often greater. Finally, the transition to civilian or veteran status presents challenges that may not be experienced in the civilian sector. When we think about military life, it's important to start with how people wind up in the military.

The Road to Membership

Viewing the road to membership in the military includes exploring why people join the military and pathways to joining the military. These decisions also involve deciding on whether to join as an enlisted member vs officer, which branch of service to join, and whether to join full time (active duty) or part-time with the National Guard or Reserves.

Why We Join

There are many reasons people join the military. We briefly cover seven main categories here: conscription, service and sense of duty, family tradition, economic betterment and opportunities, educational benefits, track to citizenship, and leave situations behind.

Conscription. Conscription is mandatory or compulsory service in the military. In the United States, the Selective Service System oversees conscription, also known as the draft into military service. All male citizens, upon turning 18 years old, are required to register with the Selective Service System. Failure to register before the age of 26 can result in denial of government benefits later in life. The last time the draft was used was during the Vietnam war. During times of peace, the US Military is comprised of an all-volunteer force. If there were a national emergency or war that could not be supported or sustained by the current military force, then Congress and the president can reinstate the draft to call up male citizens for service.

Service and Sense of Duty. Many who join the military do so out of a sense of duty and patriotism and a desire to serve their country. Sometimes this sense of duty grows from a person's participation in Junior Reserve Officer Training Corps (JROTC). Many high schools offer JROTC as an extracurricular activity, the goal of which is to instill discipline, leadership, teamwork, a sense of community service, and citizenship. These are the common goals of military training and participation in a military organization in high school can often lead to pursuing a military career once a student graduates. For others, this sense of duty can be triggered by significant national events such as Pearl Harbor in 1941 and the bombing of the World Trade Center towers on 9/11/2001. These tragic events often serve as a personal call to arms for many who are compelled to respond to a nation under attack.

Family Tradition. Service members often follow the family tradition of military service by joining themselves. Some serve in the same branch; others carve out their own path in a different branch of service. It is common for brothers and sisters, parents and children, and other relatives to serve in the military at the same time. This family tradition often stems from the value of service and sense of duty instilled in the family ethos.

Economic Betterment and Opportunities. Military service can offer steady employment and advancement opportunities. Not everyone comes from a community that has economic opportunities for its citizens. Moreover, difficult national economic times often spur people to join the military. For those who do not want to go to college or cannot afford education beyond high school, the military option offers opportunities to learn a trade and begin a new career. Young married couples sometimes see a military career as a means to economic security. Learning a trade or putting one's college education to use in the military can create financial stability for the service member and family. For those who choose to stay for 20 years, the retirement benefits can be a nice financial cushion while transitioning to a new post-military career.

Educational Benefits. As mentioned above, many high school students cannot afford to go to college. Those who have a college degree may opt to join the military so they can further their education. The military provides opportunities to go to college while in the military. Once the member leaves military service, the VA can provide educational benefits through the Post-9/11 GI Bill. Eligibility and details on how the program works can be found at the VA website (va.gov)

Another option for help with college expenses is applying for Reserve Officer Training Corps scholarship programs that exist at many colleges and universities. The ROTC program provides candidates with a college education while preparing them for a future career as a military officer. ROTC programs include the student's choice of academic major, completion of ROTC curriculum, summer camp, and finally a military commitment once the student graduates. Upon graduation, students are commissioned as second lieutenants. The active duty service commitment can range from 4 to 6 years or more depending on the job the new officer is assigned.

Track to Citizenship. Some people join the military to gain U.S. citizenship. The US Citizenship and Immigration Services website has details for this process. Awaiting citizenship after joining the military can create challenges, such as getting a security clearance. However, it does not result in automatic denial. Each person is evaluated during the security clearance process and many factors are considered. Lack of a security clearance can limit the career fields in which a person can serve and access to certain information.

Leave Situations Behind. Not everyone has a great homelife or growing up experience. Sometimes the best thing to do is to get away. Joining the military provides that opportunity for some. It may be a bad home environment, bad neighborhood, the desire to get away from bad influences. Years ago, teen-age boys in trouble with the courts were offered the opportunity to join the military instead of going to a juvenile detention center. The decision to join the military also may be a desire to better oneself, educationally and economically. Some are driven by a need to help their families. Whatever the reason, once the decision is made to join, the member must decide on the branch and the route to take (enlisted vs officer; full-time vs part time).

Which Path to Take?

Once a person decides to join the military, several questions arise. Which branch should I join? Should I enlist or apply for a commission and become an officer? Should I apply for active duty (full-time), or do I want to be part-time (Guard or Reserves) and keep my current job or keep going to school? Many factors go into the decision.

First, which branch of service should I join—Air Force, Army, Coast Guard, Marines, Navy? That depends on career interests, level of education (sometimes), which branch has openings, and sometimes which branch is offering sign-up bonuses. Of course, family tradition, as mentioned earlier, often has an influence. Second, do I choose the enlisted route vs officer commission? That decision is determined by whether the person has a college degree, which is a requirement for officer candidacy. This can also be driven by available openings. Some officer programs are career specific and recruit differently than general officer recruitment. Examples of these professional career fields are medical, legal, and chaplaincy. Of course, the option to join the military as an enlisted member rather than pursue a commission is available to those with college degrees. Lastly, a person needs to decide whether to join full time (active duty) or part-time. Part-time service takes place within the National Guard or the Reserve Forces. The Army and the Air Force are the only branches of service that have national guard units. All branches of service and the Coast Guard have Reserve units. Once a person joins the military, life for the service member and family members changes.

Military Life for the Service Member and Family

The life of a military member is replete with opportunities, changes, and challenges. It requires discipline, flexibility, and resiliency. Many find it a rewarding experience and make it a career. Some discover that it is not the life for them and leave after their first term of service. Others find their lives profoundly changed by their military service; this is a time at which social workers may intervene. The reasons people stay in the military are similar to reasons they joined—educational and economic security and advancement, service, and sense of duty. This holds true for family members as well.

Military family members, by virtue of their relation to the military member, are connected to the military institution, its culture and service. Together military members and their families encounter and respond to the many challenges of military service. Below we look at a few elements of military life that may pose a challenge for military members and their families.

Relocations

Relocations are a standard ingredient of military service. Service members start the relocation journey when they sign up for service, moving through basic training/bootcamp to technical training and on to the first duty station. These relocations can be stressful and lonely at times; it is not uncommon for service members to meet someone during initial training or at their first duty station and marry quickly to assuage that loneliness. On the other hand, some people enter military service already married. Married service members may be able to relocate their families as they attend early training; but this is an exception rather than the rule. Families typically find themselves reunited at the first duty station.

Relocation involves picking up and moving to unfamiliar places, establishing relationships, settling into new positions, finding spouse employment, and enrolling children in new schools or day care. The frequency with which military members and families relocate often depends on branch of service, rank of service member, career/job specialty, and other factors. Some military members move every couple years, yet some are fortunate to spend years in one place. Personality, attitude, life experience, and resiliency factors play a role in how well service members and families cope with relocation.

Separations

Separations occur frequently for the service member and family for many reasons. Single service members may be separated from their units and friends when they attend training schools or are assigned to special duty, or temporary duty (TDY). Separations also affect married members, their spouses, and family. Along with training school and TDYs, service members may be assigned to remote duty locations or unaccompanied tours which can take them away from family for a year or longer. For short, temporary absences, the spouse/family must carry on without the service member. When the service member is reassigned to a remote/unaccompanied location, the family might have to move off the military installation if they live there. Sometimes families opt to move back home so they have family support while the service member is gone. As with relocations, how well the military family members cope with the separation hinges on several factors including resiliency and support structure.

Deployments

Deployments are a different type of separation; they often involve an element of danger. Military members and units are deployed around the world to places known and—in the case of special operations—unknown. Some military units are on a rotational schedule, so the service member's departure and return are somewhat predictable. However, many service members receive short-notice orders that their unit is deploying. These deployments generate a host of responses from the service members and family members.

Over the years, a variety of models regarding the emotional cycle of deployment have emerged. There are three basic phases of deployment: pre-deployment, deployment, and post-deployment. Some of the models of the emotional cycle of deployment are detailed in Chapter 9. Just like the reaction to family separations, reaction to deployments often depend on family members' personalities, attitudes, life experiences, support structure, and resiliency factors. However, the element of danger adds a stressful element to the equation.

Deployments typically entail an element of danger. When service members are deployed to hostile and often remote areas of the world, communication may be hampered, stress levels may rise, and often there is the element of ambiguous loss—not knowing if or when the service member may return. If the service member is injured, he or she will be a different person upon return. Finally, if the service member is killed, there are always unanswered questions leading to ambiguous loss.

Building and Sustaining a Family

There was a time when marriage and families were discouraged within the military; however, as time evolved, so did the views about military families. We see a change in policy where a service member had to get the commander's permission to marry. We see a change in attitude from family as a distraction to the mission to viewing the family as a source of strength and stability for the service member. Moreover, we have a growing variety of family systems: traditional families with one member in the service, dual-military couples (both partners in the service), single parent families, multi-generational families, stepfamilies, and same-gender partnerships. While each family system has a unique dynamic, challenges, and strengths associated with it, they all share common elements. Every family is focused on finding the best way to navigate military life and all that encompasses.

Spouse Employment/Education

One of the greatest challenges many spouses identify is the ability to find employment or to continue their education. Frequent moves and the need to care for the children often impedes a spouse's ability to find relevant and meaningful work. Daycare and transportation issues can also impede the ability to find employment. Some licenses or specialty certificates do not transfer from state to state or to another country. To address this issue, many military installations offer spouse employment programs through their family support organizations (called by different names depending on branch of service). In addition, many companies hire employees who work from home. Finally, completing a college degree may prove difficult, especially if a spouse is enrolled in a brick-and-mortar institution, then must move. Thankfully, the move to online learning by many colleges and universities is helping to ease that challenge.

From the Children's Perspective

Children or "military brats" are an integral part of the military system. In 1986, Defense Secretary Caspar Weinberger designated April as the Month of the Military Child. This was part of the movement that recognized the importance of the military family within the military system. Programs related to this celebration highlight the contributions, sacrifices, and challenges of military children. This family-focused movement also resulted in establishing and strengthening programs for children—daycare, after school programs, youth sports programs, etc. As military families grew, researchers began to examine the effects of military life on children.

Results of studies throughout the years have noted that children are resilient and adapt easily to military life while others note that military children face all sorts of difficulties and challenges. As mentioned earlier, the ability of family members to adapt to military life depends in great part on the child's stage of development and personality, along with the parents' attitudes toward military service, their own resiliency, and the way in which a family functions as a unit. There are of course external factors that may influence a child's response to military life as well.

Children who experience frequent moves may encounter difficulties making friends and adjusting to new schools. This is especially true in the pre-teen and teen years when teens are establishing themselves socially and beginning their move from parental reliance. Ruff and Keim (2014) note additional challenges: changes in curriculum and delays in transferring records to the new school; limited eligibility and access to sports and extracurricular programs; and limited understanding of the military culture by school staff. Additionally, if the child has special needs, it may be difficult to sustain or re-establish the individual education plans (IEP) at a new location. It also may be difficult to secure the same level of supportive health care for the child. Not only do children face challenges with relocations, they also can face varied and unique challenges when a parent deploys.

There is no shortage of journal articles pertaining to the effects of deployment and a parent's battle injury on the child. What are some of the issues being explored in the research? Some studies focus on response to deployment based on the developmental stages of the child. Others examine whether there is a different reaction when a mother deploys vs a father. Those who developed the emotional cycle of deployment look at children's reactions during the stages of deployment. Additionally, boundary ambiguity and ambiguous loss are explored in the context of military deployments. These topics are easily found by conducting an internet search.

Some of the responses can be developmental regression by young children, acting out, risky behavior, anxiety, and depression in older children.

When a parent returns with issues such as post-traumatic stress (PTS) or TBI, children can develop secondary traumatic stress response. Children might also be subjected to neglect or abuse by the remaining parent or returning parent. Children of single parents may find themselves moving and living with grandparents, the other parent, or relatives while the parent is deployed. On the other hand, some children cope well with deployments and experience a strengthening of their coping ability and resiliency. Cozza and Lerner (2013) note

> the severity of the stress, the proximity of the experience, the children's age and gender, their history of exposure to other traumatic experiences, their parents' or caregivers' functional capacity, and the availability of social supports all typically contribute to the outcome (p. 5).

Understanding the effects of military life on children, the developmental levels of children and responses to stressful situations is vital to developing effective strategies and support systems for military children.

The Road to Veteran Status

Most veterans lead productive and healthy lives after their military service. For others, life after military service can be a challenge. This is especially true if the military member sustained any injury or trauma during service, developed mental health or substance abuse problems, or did not prepare adequately for separation from the military. Transitioning to civilian life and veteran status comes in many forms. It may be a simple voluntary transition from a single term of service or a 20+ year career. On the other hand, it may be a quick and unexpected transition due to health issues, getting into trouble, or military force downsizing. The nature of the discharge or release from active duty also may affect whether the service member receives adequate information regarding VA benefits and services. In this section we highlight different definitions of military veteran then cover the transition to veteran status and some of the challenges that may be encountered along the way.

Who is a Veteran?

The term veteran can be confusing. Dictionary definitions describe a veteran as someone who has *or* has had a great deal of experience in a given field. The definition implies a veteran could be someone who either is still practicing in that field or once did. Oftentimes organizations, researchers and authors use this definition of veteran to describe anyone with military experience--current (active duty, Guard, Reserve) as well as former military members (veterans). This can cause confusion; if you look for information about veterans, you may find a book or article is focused on current service members or both current and former members rather than just those who are no longer serving. In this book, ***a veteran is someone who once served, but is no longer actively engaged in military service.*** This can be a person who served one term and got out, served 20+ years and retired, or someone in between who either left voluntarily or had to leave due to medical or other reasons (involuntary separation). Anyone who once served in the military is considered a veteran.

Section 101(2) of Title 38 of the US Code, Veteran Benefits, narrows the definition a bit more by defining a veteran as "as a person who served in the active military, naval, air, or space service, and who was discharged or released therefrom *under conditions other than dishonorable* [emphasis added]" (Title 38 US Code, p. 5). The Department of Veteran Affairs uses this definition of veteran to determine eligibility for benefits. Those with service characterizations that are deemed dishonorable—other than honorable discharge, bad conduct discharge, dishonorable discharge, and dismissal (officer discharge)—are not eligible for VA benefits.

For military members who serve in the Reserves or the National Guard, veteran status can be difficult to achieve. National Guard and Reserve members who are discharged from service typically do not qualify for veteran status unless they served in active-duty status outside of training. However, during times of conflict, it is common for a National Guard or Reserve member to serve on active duty and thus be eligible for veteran status and benefits. One interesting bit of information is that veterans who previously served on active duty, then switched to service in the Guard or Reserves can apply for VA benefits. A person can still serve with a VA disability rating but can't receive both drill pay and disability payments. It's one or the other. The person must defer the VA disability payments until retirement or drill for almost no compensation. You can find additional information on this topic from the vetsfirst.org website (http://www.vetsfirst.org/reservists-national-guard-disability-compensation/).

Veterans come from all backgrounds and walks of life. They span the war generations from WWII, Korean, Vietnam, Gulf Wars and the wars in Iraq and Afghanistan. Each of these veterans may present a composite of issues unique to their experience and background. From a cultural competency perspective, it's important to remember that the veteran population in the US consists of members from five different war eras, with each generation having unique challenges related to their service. Moreover, they represent every ethnic, gender, racial, and religious category; the cultural influence of these demographics must be considered when working with veterans.

Why Military Members Leave

We started this chapter discussing reasons why people join the military. It makes sense then to consider why people leave military service as well. Some of the reasons are the same as those given for joining—pursuing new opportunities, family considerations, work stressors, and injury and its ramifications. Incompatibility with military life may also result in discharge from service.

Pursue New Opportunities, End of Career

Some people join the military and fulfill one term so they can take advantage of the VA educational benefits after leaving military service. Others find that they can make better money in the civilian sector using the technical training they've received. Additionally, civilian jobs typically do not involve danger and extensive absences from family like military careers and thus provide more family stability. Finally, many service members leave the military once they are retirement eligible. Most service members in this category successfully complete their military careers and transition to civilian life without too much difficulty.

Family Considerations

Caring for family while serving in the military is challenging. Family considerations often take center stage, especially if both members in a marriage are military. It can be difficult to balance family life if both spouses are subject to deployment. Additionally, there may be financial considerations when frequent moves prevent the civilian spouse from being able to secure employment. The strain of military life often forces a tough decision to preserve the marriage and keep the family intact.

Work Environment Stressors

Other reasons people leave the military include the stress of toxic environments (from a mental health perspective) within a military unit and operational tempo. Discrimination, hazing, and sexual harassment/attacks still exist within the military and members often leave service because of workplace harassment. Additionally, back-to-back deployments leave little time for rest and recovery or the ability to plan any aspect of life. Many leave military service because they are exhausted from the strain of repeated deployments or mental health issues due to toxic work settings.

Injury or Incompatibility

Military members may be injured during training or deployments that prevent them from continued service. Moreover, many who are injured during deployment often find themselves in trouble as they try to manage their physical injury, depression, PTS or TBI through self-medication which can lead to substance abuse, domestic abuse, workplace difficulties, etc. Additionally, there are some who fail to adapt to military life or whose behavior is not compatible with military service and are discharged for legal, financial, or other reasons. Whatever the reasons for leaving, successful transition to veteran status depends on many factors including timing (planned or unexpected exit), preparation (using available programs, setting oneself up for success), and the mental and physical health of the service member (was the member injured during military service that creates transitional challenges?).

Preparing for Veteran/Civilian Life

The key to effective transition to life as a veteran is preparation and planning. Of course, taking the necessary steps to prepare for separation from the military is easier when it is a planned departure. When the separation is involuntary due to injury, illness, or other reasons, members and their families are caught off guard and the window for preparing is shortened considerably. Furthermore, the nature of an injury or illness may require additional consideration and assistance from outside sources.

Planning for Voluntary Separation

Military members often have post-service goals and plans to achieve them while serving. However, some service members—after serving 4 years or nearing the end of a 20-year career—depart without advance preparation or a plan. Without a plan, they may flounder once they become veterans. Several agencies either mandate or offer transition assistance programs (TAP) to help service members. Service members are required to enroll in the TAP program 1 year prior to separation; however, operational requirements often make this challenging for some branches of the military. Although members are eligible to attend TAP up to 1 year after separation, many do not avail themselves of the resources that are offered through the TAP program. In late 2022, the Army instituted a pilot program, extending the preparation timeline to 2 years. The goal is to give military members additional time to participate in the program and better prepare them for the transition to civilian life (Boulin, 2023).

Transition Assistance. Both the DoD and the VA offer TAP. The DoD program is a mandated program that is provided on each military installation. The goal is to help service members and spouses make the transition to civilian life. The DoD TAP website is https://www.dodtap.mil/dodtap/app/home.

The DoD TAP consists of initial counseling, pre-separation briefing, VA and Department of Labor briefings, specialized track seminars to help meet vocational or educational goals, and a capstone session to ensure all elements have been covered. You can learn more about this program from https://www.military.com/military-transition/transition-assistance-program-overview.html. The VA TAP program also helps military members transition to civilian life and its one-day seminar focuses specifically on explaining VA benefits and services to military members getting ready to separate. It is often incorporated into the DoD TAP agenda. See https://www.benefits.va.gov/transition/tap.asp for more information. Both programs encourage service members to take advantage of the program a year ahead of separation from the military. Preparation is key to successful transition.

Enrolling in the VA System

One of the biggest and first challenges veterans face is filing disability claims. As soon as a military member separates or retires from the military, the first thing he/she should do is enroll in the VA system and file a claim with the VA. Some military installations include this service as part of the separation process. Furthermore, there are many veterans service organizations such as the Disabled American Veterans, AMVETS, American Legion, and Veterans of Foreign Wars that assist service members with this process. The VA website lists resources you can use to help you file as well. A Veterans Service Officer can assist in the claims process. This claim process, if not initiated or if delayed can have significant consequences for the veteran and family. Here is the VA website for filing a claim: https://www.va.gov/disability/get-help-filing-claim. Chapter 10 outlines the many benefits and services available to veterans from the VA. There are housing, education, burial, health, and family services available to veterans and their families.

When Separation is Unplanned or Unexpected

There are times when separation or discharge from military service is unplanned or unexpected. Illness, injury, military force downsizing, or disciplinary issues may lead to a discharge. When this occurs, there is little time to prepare or plan. In the case of injury or illness, additional resources may be required to care for the service member and assist the family in the transition to civilian life. Knowledge and access to these services are critical for successful departure from the military. It is often these situations that leave a military member and family vulnerable to financial, housing, legal, and mental health troubles setting in motion a cascade of difficulties. It may take several years for a veteran or family to regain stability. Worst case scenario: substance abuse, homelessness, family violence, or suicide can result from an inability to overcome the lack of adequate planning prior to leaving the military and to secure resources to cope with the challenges.

Military life can be a great adventure. It can also be a challenging journey. Each service member's and family member's experience is different. Military service is not always pretty. Understanding daily life as well as life for those who deploy often is critical to effective social work practice. Some military veterans have seen more than their fair share of battle and then there are veterans who served for 25 years, but never deployed. That does not mean life wasn't stressful; it is just a different type of stress. Each branch of service participates in, and experiences deployments and battles differently yet battle wounds and the residuals of military service have similar characteristics. We look at some of the ramifications of military service throughout the remaining chapters.

Final Thoughts

There are many pathways to membership in the military. People consider their reasons for joining and the nature of their membership (full time or part time, which branch, officer or enlisted, etc.; and how long to stay) when deciding to join. Military service provides financial stability, opportunities to live all over the world, and structured environments with built-in resources for family members. However, the unique aspects of military life for families involve frequent moves and separations, deployments and the risk of danger, and challenges pertaining to spouse employment and education, and child development. Finally, the journey to veteran status varies for each military member: reasons for leaving, time served, how military service influences the decision to leave, and how well the service member navigates the transition. Preparation, planning, and using available resources are key to effective transition to veteran/civilian life.

References

Boulin, B. (2023). *Army transition assistance program is extending its timeline for soldiers.* My Base Guide. https://mybaseguide.com/army-transition-assistance-program/

Cozza, S. J., & Lerner, R. M. (Fall, 2013). Military children and families: Introducing the issue. *The Future of Children, 23(2).* www.futureofchildren.org

Pincus, S. H., House, R., Christensen, J., & Adler, L. E. (2005). The emotional cycle of deployment: A military family perspective. *US Army Medical Department Journal, 4(5).*

Ruff, S. B., & Keim, M. A. (2014). Revolving doors: The impact of multiple school transitions on military children. *The Professional Counselor, 4*(2), 103–113. https://doi.org/10.15241/sbr.4.2.103

Title 38 U. S. Code—Veterans' Benefits. (2011). Government Printing Office.

Vets First. (2015). *Can Reservists and National Guard Members receive VA Disability Compensation?* Retrieved from http://www.vetsfirst.org/reservists-national-guard-disability-compensation/

Effect of Deployments and Battle on Service Members
CHAPTER FOUR

In Chapter 3, we mentioned deployments briefly. Here we look at the nature of deployments and their effect on service members. We explore the types of deployments, the inherent risks of them, and the physical and psychological fallout of deployments, especially those that involve battle. Each type of injury presented here is covered in more detail in the ensuing chapters.

What is a deployment? Deployments are the movement of personnel and equipment to another location to perform military duties. The Department of Defense (DoD) Dictionary of Military and Associated Terms (2021) defines deployment as "the movement of forces into and out of an operational area" (p. 62). As hot spots around the world intensify, so does the need for deployed forces, which in turn strains day-to-day operations at home station as well as family and community relationships. Units may deploy for training, humanitarian, peacekeeping/security, or combat missions. Here in the US recently, National Guard and Reserve units have been deployed to assist during national disasters, assist in numerous ways with the Covid-19 pandemic, and to quell protests and riots in several cities. The level of danger or potential for injury depends on the nature of the mission.

Some deployments are scheduled and predictable while others may crop up without warning and with little time to prepare. Service members and families are better able to cope with deployments when they have time to prepare logistically and psychologically for separation. Additionally, deployments vary in length. For example, training deployments may only be a few weeks, while combat missions may last a year. This was especially true after 9/11. Deployments became longer, more frequent, and more dangerous. The longer and more dangerous the deployment, the greater the strain on the service member and family, especially in terms of reintegration. Finally, active duty, guard, and reserve units are all subject to deployment; however, support systems for the different military branches are not the same. The cycle of deployment, covered in Chapter 9, has emotional, psychological, and behavioral consequences for the service member and family.

Separations

All deployments involve separation from family and friends. Separations are a natural part of military service. From day one, the service member is separated from familiar surroundings and people for bootcamp/basic training and then training unique to their chosen military occupation. Each subsequent assignment may bring separation as well. For example, Navy personnel serving on ships or submarines may find themselves away from home for 6 months or more. Deployments, depending on the mission, may mean separation for a few weeks or a year or more.

Along with separation from family and friends, deployments interrupt service members' career and educational goals. This is especially true for Guard and Reserve members who may have civilian careers or for service members who are taking college courses. Deployments put those aspirations on hold. If the service member is injured in any way, those aspirations may be on hold permanently.

Communication before, during, and after deployment influences the ability to deal with the pre-deployment, deployment, and post-deployment process. When military members and their families have open communication, they are better able to prepare for departure and the attendant emotions. Service members and families get through the deployment better if the service member can communicate with family during the deployment; however, the nature and dangers of the deployment may make communicating honestly more difficult or may put additional worry and strain on the family. Communication post deployment can be affected by such factors as length of time away, poor communication prior to deployment, unwillingness to share the deployment experience with family, and injuries/trauma that may hinder the service member's ability to communicate.

Reintegration and reunification with family members can be difficult for many service members. The effectiveness with which the reintegration occurs depends on many factors including the nature of the service member's and family's response to the deployment, whether there was any injury or traumatic event, and the resiliency of both the service member and family members to deal with the effects of the deployment.

Deployment Risks

Deployments over the decades exposed military members to hazardous and austere conditions which have a lasting effect on military members' physical, psychological, and spiritual health. Service members endure combat, enemy assaults and attacks, dangerous convoys and outposts, exposure to hazmat and unhealthy environmental conditions (poor diet, lack of sleep, extreme weather), family separation, death of fellow service members, disruption of career and educational plans, etc. Unfortunately, military service sometimes involves attacks and injury from fellow service members—bullying, harassment, abuse, and sexual assault to name a few. As a result, many service members find themselves facing physical, emotional, psychological, and neurological challenges that may last a lifetime and have a profound effect on the member and families (Blaisure et al., 2016).

Advances in protective personal protection gear and battlefield triage and treatment meant more service members survived wounds that normally would result in death. Additionally, advanced, mobile hospitals and critical care units near the battlefront also save lives. However, surviving horrific wounds comes at a cost.

Some of the recent military operations include:

First Gulf War/Persian Gulf War, also known as Operation Desert Shield/Desert Storm took place between 2 August 1990 and 28 February 1991. Phase 1, Operation Desert Shield consisted of the buildup of troops and equipment followed by Operation Desert Storm which was the combat phase. When Iraq invaded and annexed Kuwait 2 August 1990 in response to rising oil prices and production disputes, 35 nations joined US forces and stepped in to fight Saddam Hussein's forces.

Operation Enduring Freedom (OEF)—Actions in Afghanistan Oct 7, 2001 – Dec 31, 2014—is the official name for the Global War on Terrorism (GWOT) as a result of the 9-11 bombing of the Twin Towers in NYC.

Operation Iraqi Freedom (OIF)—Actions in Iraq March 2003-Aug 2010.

OIF was launched in response to Iraq's refusal to abide by the United Nations Security Council's many resolutions to allow UN inspectors to verify that Iraq did not possess weapons of mass destruction (WMD) and ballistic missiles.

Operation New Dawn (OND)—Actions, Dec 2010-Dec 2011, to advise, assist, and train Iraqi security forces in the rebuilding of their country.

The Defense Casualty Analysis System, https://dcas.dmdc.osd.mil/dcas/pages/casualties.xhtml, lists each military engagement and the casualties incurred by service members in these military engagements along with the other wars that the US has participated in. This site only lists deaths, injuries and whether the injury required hospitalization by branch of service; however, no details on specific injuries are mentioned.

Each war or military engagement has its unique battle challenges and injuries. For example, veterans from the Vietnam era still fight to get recognition, compensation, and treatment for Agent Orange and radiation related illnesses. While those who were in Vietnam finally got some government assistance through the VA, many who worked on the Navy ships that carried the poison (Blue Water Navy ships) and those (military and civilian) who were in the test areas (e.g.: Eglin Reservation, FL,

Effect of Deployments and Battle on Service Members

1962-1970) are still fighting for compensation and recognition. Service members from the first Gulf War (1990-1991) battle residual effects from Gulf War Syndrome or Illness, a chronic and multi-symptom disorder that affects the physical and psychological health of service members caused by exposure to the burn pits. Gulf War Syndrome can cause chronic fatigue, cognitive problems, rashes, to name a few conditions. Some research found this condition passed to children and spouses much like Agent Orange. The 2022 PACT Act directs the VA to treat over 20 **presumptive** illnesses and conditions believed to be related to toxic exposure. Furthermore, additional Agent Orange and radiation locations have been added to the list of eligible service assignments. Finally, this law will bring long overdue compensation and treatment to Vietnam, Gulf War, and post-9/11 veterans. The term presumptive is important; veterans will not have to prove exposure to toxic conditions to be eligible for compensation for these related conditions. Additionally, the Anthrax vaccine is often blamed for compromised immune systems during this first Gulf War period. Finally, PTSD and TBI have been labeled the signature wounds of the OEF/OIF/second Gulf War era because of their prevalence among service members.

Physical Injury

Physical injury is a natural part of military service. Injuries occur right from the start—basic training/boot camp, technical or job training—then the physical strain of daily training and inherent dangers of deployment. Army soldiers and Marines spend most of their time in battle training. Certain occupational specialties are physically demanding—Army Rangers and Green Beret, Navy Seals, Marine Raiders, Air Force Special Tactics and Pararescue personnel, Coast Guard Special Forces—just to name a few. Carrying heavy loads, jumping out of airplanes and the rigors of daily training can result in sprains, strains, fractures, and broken bones. Repeated injury can result in chronic pain that the service member may not want to acknowledge or treat lest it jeopardize their career.

Physical injuries are an inherent risk in battle. There are typical sprains, strains, and broken bones, but there are also the more serious burns and disfigurements; loss of eyesight and hearing; damage to internal organs and loss of functioning, loss of limbs and appendages, and spinal cord and brain injuries. We cover these in more detail in Chapter 5.

Psychological (Invisible) Injuries

Psychological injuries are labeled invisible because they cannot be seen. There are no physical manifestations of these conditions, such as visible wounds, scars, or prosthetics. The three most common invisible wounds recognized by the DoD and VA include traumatic brain injury (TBI), post-traumatic stress disorder (PTS/PTSD), and major depressive disorder (MDD). Although traumatic brain injury is considered an invisible wound, it straddles the line between physical and psychological injury. It is physical damage to the brain that can have a profound effect on the cognitive and psychological functioning of the service member.

Psychological injuries encompass a continuum of responses to the stress of military service. Stress associated with battle is termed combat stress reaction (CSR) these days, but over the years it has had many names such as shell shock, nervous exhaustion, and battle fatigue. Categories of combat stress reaction include PTS/PTSD, acute stress reaction (ASR), and combat and operational stress response (COSR). Other responses to combat stress include MDD, substance use disorder (SUD), and anxiety conditions such as General Anxiety Disorder (GAD).

Stress response (the concept of fight, flight, or freeze) is necessary for survival. Combat stress reaction ranges from healthy response and functioning to maladaptive responses. Exposure to prolonged, repeated stress drains individuals' stores of resiliency which can eventually have a negative effect on day-to-day functioning. Some of these maladaptive responses can manifest in the following ways: risky and dangerous behavior; thrill seeking; addiction to alcohol, drugs, gambling, and sex; and anger issues such as road rage (Blaisure et al., 2016) We take a closer look at invisible wounds in Chapter 6.

Moral Injury

Moral injury results when actions or behaviors run counter to service members' ethical, moral, or religious foundations. This can result from a person's own decisions or actions or the actions and decisions of leaders and others. Moral injury manifests as guilt, shame, loss of faith or trust in authority and institutions, and/or disillusionment. Other signs include social isolation, lack of concern or empathy for others, loss of a spiritual connection, and loss of self-worth (Blaisure et al. 2016). We explore moral injury further in Chapter 7.

Response to Deployments and Related Injuries

Dealing with deployments and related injuries covers a broad spectrum of challenges and responses. From the psychological effects of separation and reunion, injury, and loss, to the challenges of coping with physical injuries and recovery, and the often spiritual or moral angst service members may develop, service members may find themselves facing daunting hurdles. One of the first hurdles is the homecoming after a deployment.

Post-deployment: reunion, reintegration, renegotiation

Post-deployment or redeployment is filled with myriad and often conflicting emotions: anticipation, joy, fear, anxiousness, sadness, to name a few. For most coming home is a time of excitement because the service member is reunited with family and back on familiar territory. As the excitement of being back home subsides, the task of reintegrating into the family begins. Time does not stand still for either the deploying member or the family members at home. People change during deployments; those at home gain new skills and newfound independence. The transition back to family requires some adjustment and often some renegotiation of roles each member will assume now that the family unit is intact.

Coping with the Deployment Experience

Depending on the nature of the deployment, some service members will have few negative responses to the experience other than missing family and friends at home or having to delay personal goals. On the other hand, the deployment may have such a profound effect on service members that they may seem vastly different from the person they were prior to deployment. This may be due to physical, psychological, or moral injury during the deployment. Furthermore, service members may be unable or unwilling to communicate the effect of the deployment on their well-being to their family members, straining family relations to varying degrees. Communication is vital during the deployment cycle; if something happens that the service member does not wish to communicate with others, it can influence the entire communication process. And what if the service member sustains a physical injury that affects the ability to communicate?

These physical, psychological, and moral injuries may leave the service member with long rehabilitation periods or with limited ability to perform daily activities. Relationships at work and at home may be strained if the service member acquired PTSD, a mild TBI, or develops depression. These conditions often lead to substance abuse as a coping mechanism or legal problems which carry their own set of difficulties. If the service member can no longer perform military duties, separation from the service leads to another path of challenges and difficulties for the military family—logistical, financial, medical, and legal. We explore the fallout of deployment more fully in the subsequent chapters.

Addressing Military Health Issues

As DoD institutions and families acknowledge and better understand the effect military service has on the service member and families, policies, and programs—both government and community—emerge to respond to the challenges. Health professionals from all disciplines find themselves working with military members—past and present—and their families. The need to understand the military experience becomes vital in the health professionals' quest for cultural competency as well as competency in their own discipline. The need for culturally competent health care providers is seen throughout

Effect of Deployments and Battle on Service Members

the VA, DoD, and individual service branches. Community and not-for-profit organizations have also proliferated in response to the need for assistance. One response to the need for more information can be found with the VA.

The VA Health Initiative was established in 2014 to provide practitioners information and resources so they may better serve military members and veterans. The 15 individual study courses have been replaced with individual links to updated and current information at this website (Note: Some of the topics are better covered and more helpful than others): https://www.publichealth.va.gov/vethealthinitiative/

Some of the less well-known topics include agent orange, infectious Southwest Asia diseases, Gulf War Syndrome, radiation exposure, cold weather injuries, POW issues. The more common topics include TBI, PTSD, military sexual trauma, and battle wounds.

The VA also established Centers of Excellence to provide specialized care for specific conditions such as PTSD, TBI, spinal cord injury (SCI), geriatric issues and more. These centers provide comprehensive and specialized care for veterans and their families. The DoD developed and mandated that other programs be offered at military installations as well.

To help families navigate military service, the DoD requires military installations to have family advocacy and readiness programs on each installation. These programs provide a vast array of services to assist military family members with the stressors of daily life. Education, deployment preparation and reunification, special needs programs, domestic violence prevention, and transition assistance are the most common of these programs. Individual military branches and installations may offer additional programs based on the needs of their members and families. For example, the Warrior Care Recovery Coordination Program, operated by the Defense Health Agency, assists wounded military members. Each branch of service has an affiliate organization: AF Wounded Warrior Program, Army Recovery Care Program, Navy Wounded Warrior, and Marine Wounded Warrior Regiment. More information can be found at https://warriorcare.dodlive.mil/About/

Community programs exist as well. There are service related organizations such as American Legion and Veterans of Foreign Wars. There are enlisted and officer organizations as well that advocate for the service members and veterans. Other organizations include Disabled American Veterans and Paralyzed Veterans of America that provide services and advocacy assistance to veterans and transitioning service members and families. Organizations that specialize in housing for veterans also exist: Habitat for Humanity, the Gary Sinise Foundation RISE program, Operation Finally Home, Homes for Our Troops, Building Homes for Heroes, to name a few. Finally, there are many churches and local organizations that offer programs specifically for military members and families.

Daily life for the service member can be stressful, and deployments, especially those to dangerous locations, take their toll on everyone, sometimes with dire consequences. The DoD, VA, and community organizations are continuously creating innovative programs to assist service members and families with the cycle of military service. Is the system perfect? No. Are health professionals fully knowledgeable and prepared to tackle the many facets of military life that add layers to a client's case? No. Only through research, education, and implementation of evolving programs can we hope to achieve success. The following chapters provide a steppingstone for your academic and professional journey into military social work.

Final Thoughts

Deployments are the movement of personnel and equipment to another location to perform military duties. Deployments are a natural part of military life and often have an element of risk associated with them. Deployments take a toll on both the service member and the family. Dealing with separations, reunions, and injuries and their aftermath all require a support system to navigate through the emotional and logistical aspects. Furthermore, deployments can result in injury—physical, invisible (psychological), and moral. Dealing with these injuries is difficult; treating these injuries require special knowledge, skills, and abilities. Moreover, coping with the deployment experience hinges on effective communication among family members and is the focus of many interventions.

The Department of Defense and its military branches along with the Veterans Health Administration work to address current issues associated with military service. Through research and development of programs and interventions, the needs of service members are being addressed. Additionally, community programs and not-for-profit organizations strive to complement government programs for service members, veterans and their families.

References
Blaisure, K. R., Saathoff-Wells, T., Pereira, A., Wadsworth, S. M., & Dombro, A. L. (2016). *Serving military families, 2nd ed.* Routledge.
Defense Casualty Analysis System. (n.d.). https://dcas.dmdc.osd.mil/dcas/pages/casualties.xhtml
Deployment. (2021). Department of defense (DoD) dictionary of military and associated terms. https://irp.fas.org/doddir/dod/dictionary.pdf

Physical Injuries
CHAPTER FIVE

Physical wounds include the spectrum from injuries incurred from training and carrying heavy loads to loss of limb(s) and functionality due to accidents and battle. Categories of physical wounds include but are not limited to stress and strain injuries, loss of limbs, burns and disfigurements, spinal cord injuries, and loss of sight and hearing. Physical wounds often involve mental and emotional scarring as well. Over the decades, advances in medicine and battle wound treatment have had a profound effect on the survival of wounded service members. Preventing infection and ways to prevent bleeding to death were some of the first advances. The combination and employment of advanced field medicine, triage techniques, and quick evacuations were key strategies to improving survival rates on the battlefield (Barnes, 2022). Highly advanced mobile field hospitals were also critical in saving lives. In this chapter we highlight the most common military injuries. We look at physical injury as an occupational hazard, common military injuries from each military engagement, and summarize several types of physical injuries your clients may have because of their military experience.

Physical Injury as an Occupational Hazard

Every occupation has some level of risk associated with it and the military is no different. The physical demands of military service put service members at risk of injury from day one in basic training/bootcamp. According to the Army Public Health Center (2022), musculoskeletal injuries caused by single sudden events and repeated stress and overuse of are the greatest contributors to physical injury of service members. These training related injuries include strains, sprains of the lower extremities from physical fitness training, running and marching, shoulder and back injuries from carrying and lifting heavy loads. Road marching injuries include stress fractures, back, foot and knee pain from carrying heavy loads, foot blisters that can become infected and debilitating. Injury may also occur during obstacle courses and combat training. Advanced job training for specific military occupational specialties may result in additional injury or chronic overuse. Parachuting and survival training also adds an element of risk for physical injury. Motor vehicle accidents, falls, and sports injuries are common both on duty and off duty. Finally, it is common for military members to experience vision and hearing injuries as an occupational hazard. When service members are deployed, there are additional risks and hazards, some life-taking and some life-altering.

Prevalent Injuries by Conflict

Each military conflict entails injuries unique to that engagement. Disease and infection, amputations, and bullet/shrapnel wounds were the main culprits of the American Civil War. Mustard gas was the signature weapon of World War I along with extreme cold weather exposure, bullets, and shrapnel. World War II service members (September 1, 1939 – September 2, 1945) were also exposed to mustard gas and extreme cold weather. Additionally, they were exposed to ionizing radiation from nuclear weapons testing and hazardous materials associated with their jobs. Exposure to loud noises was common as well. During the Korean War (June 25, 1950 – July 27, 1953) service members experienced similar injuries as previous conflicts—hazardous material exposure, cold weather injuries, radiation and iodizing radiation exposure, asbestos exposure, and noise. The Vietnam War (November 1, 1965 – April 30, 1975) saw a repeat of most of the previous hazards (VA, 2021). Agent Orange was the signature weapon of that conflict and had long-term effects on US military members. This defoliant resulted in myriad health issues for service members and civilians alike that would take years for the government and Veterans Affairs to respond. It wasn't until the Agent Orange Act of 1991 established presumptive service connection for veterans who served during *certain time periods in specific locations* that there was any acknowledgement or right to file disability claims with the VA. Even then, the act restricted compensation for those who were in Vietnam. Many Air Force members stationed in Thailand and Navy personnel on ships were not eligible for compensation despite being exposed to Agent Orange.

More recent conflicts such as the First Gulf War (Operations Desert Shield and Desert Storm) and the Iraq and Afghanistan Conflicts (Operation Iraqi Freedom/Operation New Dawn and Operation Enduring Freedom, respectively) saw new and unique threats to physical health. While earlier conflicts exposed service members to extreme cold weather, these conflicts exposed service members to extreme heat and desert conditions. Members deployed in support of the First Gulf War were exposed to burning oil fields, chemical and biological weapons, along with depleted uranium. These exposures left many with unexplained illnesses that would later be dubbed Gulf War Syndrome or Gulf War Illness, a chronic and multi-symptom disorder with devasting effects. The ensuing conflicts in Iraq and Afghanistan saw similar injury/illness due to desert conditions. Add to these several SW Asian infectious diseases such as malaria, mycobacterium tuberculosis, nontyphoid salmonella, shigella, visceral leishmaniasis, and West Nile Virus to name a few. The signature injury of the Gulf War Conflicts is traumatic brain injury (TBI) mostly from Improvised Explosive Devices (IED) used by the enemy against convoys and encampments (VA, 2021).

Types of Physical Battle Injuries

In this section we briefly describe the main physical injuries military members may sustain while deployed and engaged in battle. This is not an all-inclusive list, just a few to start the conversation and encourage further research.

Physical Injuries

Blast Injuries

When we think of battle wounds, what typically comes to mind first are bullet wounds. While this was certainly the most common battle wound in past conflicts, warfare has emerged to include longer-range attacks on personnel and targets. Blast injuries—the result of explosions and include shrapnel injuries—have become one of the leading causes of military injury. According to the Centers for Disease Control (CDC) (2021), there are 4 classifications of blast injuries: primary, secondary, tertiary, and quaternary. Primary blast injuries are the result of over-pressurization shock waves that damage lungs, eyes, eardrums, and internal organs. Secondary blast injuries are caused by flying debris. Penetrating injuries are most often caused by shrapnel. Shrapnel is the term used to describe sharp fragments or shards from a bomb, shell, explosion, or gunfire. Shrapnel comes from the explosives themselves or from timed devices such as land mines and smart bombs. Shrapnel pierce the body and its organs, often creating damage to tissue and bones. While some shrapnel injuries result in only minor scarring, others can cause extensive damage, infection, and life-long debilitation. Some shrapnel can lodge in areas where it cannot be removed such as in the spine or brain. These wounds can cause limited functionality and difficulty with daily living tasks. Tertiary blast injuries are caused by being thrown through the air by the blast. This can cause fractures, traumatic amputation, and brain injuries. Finally, quaternary injuries are those injuries that are not covered by the first three categories. These can include infections or other conditions resulting from the blast injury. Included in this category are breathing issues such as COPD, crush injuries, and burns (CDC, 2021).

Blast Injury Burns

The development and frequent use of explosive and incendiary devices in recent conflicts led to an increase in blast injury burns incurred by military members. These burn injuries can be superficial, or they can be extensive enough to damage lungs and other organs. These burns are often one of a complex collection of injuries—shards of glass, eardrum, eye and lung damage, traumatic amputation—to name a few. Although protective armor has improved survival rates against shrapnel and bullets, they are not successful in protecting the body from burns that result from some weaponry. Atiyeh et al. (2007) note that at the time of their research, 63% of all combat burns were the result of explosive devices.

Pain and disfigurement are the primary characteristics of burn injuries. Recovery from blast burn injuries is long, complicated, and extremely painful. Even after the healing process, long-term pain due to restriction of movement is present. Scarring and disfigurement results in both physical and psychological pain and adjustment. The injury and the recovery process take a toll on the service member and the family.

The United States Army Institute of Surgical Research Burn Center (Brooke Army Medical Center; now part of Joint Base San Antonio) consists of a comprehensive team of 300 professionals solely responsible for the treatment, rehabilitation, and reintegration into the community of military members who sustain burns in combat (US Army Institute, 2021).

Traumatic Amputation and Loss of Limbs/Function

Traumatic amputation is the loss of a limb or appendage due to an accident. Most traumatic amputations in the military are the result of vehicle accidents or from blast injuries. Wallace (2012) notes that improvised explosive devices (IED) along with mortar fire and rocket propelled grenades account for 89% of traumatic amputations. Since body armor is geared toward protecting the head and torso, the extremities are vulnerable to injury. Surgical amputations are often necessary when damage to the limb or appendage cannot be repaired. In a study of functional outcome of veterans with upper extremity amputation vs limb salvage, Mitchell et al. (2019) found that both groups reported diminished levels of physical and psychosocial ability and that there was no significant difference in outcomes. Both groups faced challenges with PTSD, depression, and chronic pain; however, in this study two-thirds of participants were working or in school, and 39% were involved in sports and rigorous recreational activities.

Military personnel with traumatic amputation tend to have more comorbidities than other injuries. Not only do they have similar mental health conditions that accompany other military injuries such as post-traumatic stress, depression, and anxiety, they often develop medical conditions such as nerve damage, recurring infections, and musculoskeletal diseases. Amputees also have challenges with day-to-day functioning.

Addressing the ability to carry out activities of daily living is critical in maintaining independence. Prosthetics, mobility devices, and adaptive technology all play a key role in promoting daily functioning and independence. In addition to physical aids, it's important to consider the psychological aspects to recovery and functioning. Carter (2012) studied six Army women with limb loss and found that the women's primary concerns were accepting their new body image, being able to protect themselves, and the grieving process involved in losing a limb. Successfully coping with these concerns involved drawing upon their strength and mental training as military members, positive attitudes and a sense of humor, resiliency, and having a strong support system. Armstrong et al. echo these results in their 2018 study. They looked at the influence of variables such as resilience and personality, and employment on veterans' rehabilitation and function. The results of their study show a positive relationship between resilience and pain management, social engagement, and use of their prosthetics. Use of well-fitting prosthetics promoted a return to work and social activities. All these factors contribute to veterans having meaning and purpose in their lives.

The VA Office of Research and Development website has information about various initiatives aimed at limb loss and the development of prosthetic aids. https://www.research.va.gov/topics/prosthetics.cfm

Organ Damage and Loss of Functionality

Military members often sustain injury to external and internal organs such as eyes, ears, intestinal and reproductive organs; however, there isn't much discussion about these types of injuries. Often, diminished hearing and vision is a function of age, so when working with older veterans, these may be an added challenge for all concerned.

Vision. Vision loss in older Veterans can result from conditions such as glaucoma, cataracts, stroke, and diabetes. Vision injury can also be an occupational risk. For example, blast injuries cause damage such as blurred vision, double vision, sensitivity to light, and difficulty reading. Vision loss can also coincide with TBI (VA ORD, 2023c). Finally, computer work and work around hazardous materials or in austere conditions can affect eyesight. Deployments to desert locations expose personnel to sandstorms that can cause injury to the eyes.

Hearing. Prolonged exposure to loud noises and blasts can result in hearing loss and tinnitus. Hearing loss is the most common service-connected disability among veterans. Over 1.3 million veterans receive disability pay for hearing loss; 2.3 million received disability pay for tinnitus. Military members may sustain damage to the middle ear (conductive hearing loss) or inner ear (sensorineural hearing loss). Those exposed to jet propulsion fuel and blast injuries can also suffer from auditory processing disorder, making it difficult to understand speech. Additionally, tinnitus may be a contributing factor to positive screening for PTSD, depression, and anxiety (VA ORD, 2023a).

Genitourinary Injury. Improved protective gear and advanced and rapid medical intervention result in military members surviving injuries that would have resulted in death in earlier decades. Military members are surviving genitourinary injuries at levels never reported before. These injuries are most often caused by ground-based explosives such as IEDs, mines, etc. resulting in a constellation of injuries called dismounted complex blast injury. This type of injury causes traumatic amputation, pelvic fractures, and damage to the genitourinary organs. These types of injuries require immediate medical intervention, genital surgery, and reconstruction. Sexual dysfunction and infertility are often byproducts of these injuries (Balzano & Hudak, 2018).

Physical Injuries

Spinal Cord Injuries

Military members incur spinal cord injuries (SCI) during normal training as well as in battle. Paratroopers and those who carry heavy loads are at risk of SCI. Vehicle accidents, explosions, and gun fire also can result in SCI. The chronic pain from less severe forms of spinal injury often lead to difficulty in employment, problems with self-medication and addiction, and issues of depression. At the other end of the spectrum, the most severe form of SCI can result in full time care of the service members at home or in a treatment facility.

According to Fyffe et al. (2019), there are approximately 42,000 military veterans living with SCI who are eligible for VA care. Moreover, there are many who never sought VA participation and compensation. The long-term implications for SCI cover a broad range of limitations and effects on the individual, family, and the military institution. SCIs can result in chronic pain affecting day-to-day functioning and ability to perform job related duties. If the SCI is severe, it can result in separation from the military and loss of family income or full-time care giving responsibilities by family members. There is a cost to the military as well when highly trained personnel are no longer available to perform the mission.

Kessler et al.'s (2021) researched the incidence of SCI among US Army Special Forces. They found that Army Special Forces constitute 60% of all Special Forces casualties, due to the hazardous nature of their missions and extended combat. The cause of the injuries and the use of body armor was of particular interest to the researchers. Although only 19% of those surveyed responded, their findings reveal that airborne operations, especially landings, were the primary cause of SCIs. Moreover, although use of protective equipment such as headgear and body armor increased after 9/11; 87% reported wearing headgear, but only 36% of respondents reported wearing body armor. Finally, the researchers noted that only 16% of those sustaining an SCI were medevac'd for treatment; the lack of medical intervention in remote locations adds to the inability to quickly treat and manage SCIs in combat locations.

The DoD Congressionally Directed Medical Research Programs (2021) notes the rate of SCIs between 2000 and 2009 was about eight times that of SCIs in the civilian population. Although the incidence of SCI in the military was considered low, the VA as the largest single military SCI care network, was providing services for 10%–20% of all individuals living with an SCI in the US. In response, Congress established the Spinal Cord Injury Research Program.

Some of the physical consequences of SCI include loss of limb function; loss of organ function (bowel/urinary/erectile); cardiac disease, infections, arthritis, and tinnitus to name a few. Kessler et al. (2021) note psychological comorbidities include posttraumatic stress disorder, major depressive disorder, and generalized anxiety disorder.

Great strides are being made in the treatment and rehabilitation of military members with spinal cord injury. For example, exoskeleton suits have been created to help people walk. No longer limited to wheelchairs, this device makes it possible for greater independence and mobility. Stem cell research is also making a mark on spinal cord injury recovery. New interventions by Northwestern University include injectable "dancing molecules" that show great promise in reversing paralysis and repairing spinal tissue (Morris, 2021). You can listen to the NPR Science Friday podcast about this research here: https://www.sciencefriday.com/segments/drug-reverses-paralysis/

In addition to the scientific breakthroughs, the VA has 24 medical centers in the United States with specialized centers (called Spinal Cord Injury Centers) for Veterans with spinal cord injuries and disorders along with 5 Spinal Cord Injury (SCI) Centers that provide long term care for Veterans with SCI/D. The VA also partners with several organizations to research and provide advanced treatments to veterans with SCI (VA ORD, 2023b). Here are highlights from the VA Office of Research and Development website (https://www.research.va.gov/topics/sci.cfm)

Physical Injuries

- The VA is a member of the Paralyzed Veterans of America Consortium for Spinal Cord Medicine. The consortium evaluates current research and recommends evidence-based interventions to health care providers.
- The VA Advanced Platform Technology (APT) Center strives to counter issues veterans face related to the sensory or motor systems, cognitive deficits, or limb loss. The goal is to apply emerging technologies--prosthetics and orthotics, wireless health monitoring/maintenance, manipulating the nervous system with internal/external devices—to give veterans greater control over their bodies.
- The VA's Center for Functional Electrical Stimulation (FES), Cleveland, develops ways to use electrical stimulation to modulate nervous system activity (suppress or activate) to help move or control muscle movement in limbs or organ function such as bladder control or breathing.
- The Human Research Engineering Laboratories (HERL), Pittsburg, works to improve mobility of veterans with SCI through clinical research in medical rehabilitation and engineering.

Traumatic Brain Injury

Traumatic Brian Injury (TBI) straddles the line between physical and invisible injuries. TBI is a physical injury; however, it has been dubbed an invisible injury since the injury cannot be seen by others. As such, others often don't understand the symptoms and results of the injury, especially when it is a mild or moderate brain injury.

TBI is one of the most prevalent battle injuries of recent times. TBIs are categorized based on diagnostic criteria of loss of consciousness (LOC) and the Glasgow Coma Scale, which assigns a numeric value to a person's response to directions to a) open eyes, b) give verbal response, and c) give a physical response. These results inform the characterization of the TBI—mild, moderate, and severe. The severity of the TBI have implications for the degree of service members' ability to carry out activities of daily living (ADL) and the degree to which they require care by others.

Types of TBI include a) contusions or bruises, b) hematomas (bleeds in the brain), c) skull fractures, d) diffuse axonal injuries (tears in the nerve fibers in the brain), and e) concussions that can result in loss of consciousness, memory, confusion, headaches, etc.

Mild TBI (mTBI) is the most frequently experienced TBI in the military. It is also the one that goes unreported and undetected most often. This type of injury frequently resolves on its own after a few weeks or months; however, many service members experience lingering symptoms for years without resolution. Changes that result from TBI include

- Physical/neurological—headaches and vision, hearing, and language difficulties
- Cognitive—memory, executive functioning (planning and organizing, decision-making, concentration, self-regulation)
- Psychological—anxiety and depression, irritability, short-tempered, emotional lability
- Behavioral—decreased inhibition, risky behavior, impulse control issues, lack of empathy

More details pertaining to TBI are in the next chapter.

Recovering from physical injuries can present a challenge and sometimes extensive recovery. Some injuries are so severe that a return to original functioning is not possible. Recovery and rehabilitation depend on factors such as

- Type of injury and how it occurred
- Severity of the injury and location on the brain
- Co-occurring conditions
- Individual and family response to injury
- Available treatments and resources

Final Thoughts

Physical wounds include the spectrum from injuries incurred from training and carrying heavy loads to loss of limb(s) and functionality due to accidents and battle. The physical demands of military service put service members at risk of injury from day one in basic training/bootcamp. Each military conflict has signature injuries, from extreme weather conditions to exposure to hazardous chemicals, to PTSD and TBIs. Current era physical injuries include blast injuries, burns, organ damage, loss of limb and appendages, spinal cord injuries, and TBIs. Physical injuries can have a profound effect on service members' daily functioning, family functioning, and healthy interpersonal relationships. Recovery depends on factors such as the type and severity of the injury, co-occurring conditions, individual and family response and resiliency, and available treatments and resources. Practitioners and students are encouraged to research details about the various injuries and learn about existing and emerging treatments/interventions to help deal with and recover from military injuries.

References

Army Public Health Center. (2022). *Military activity related injuries.* https://phc.amedd.army.mil/topics/discond/ptsaip/Pages/Military-Activity-Related-Injuries.aspx

Atiyeh, B., Gunn, S., and Heyak, S. (2007). Military and civilian burn injuries during armed conflicts. *Ann Burns Fire Disasters, 20*(4), 203-215. https://www.ncbi.nlm.nih.gov/pmc/articles/PMC3188083/

Balzano, F. L., & Hudak, S. J. (2018). Military genitourinary injuries: past, present, and future. *Translational Andrology and Urology, 7*(4). 646-652.

Barnes, S. D. (2022). *Overview of physical wounds* [Module overview]. Canvas. https://wnmu.instructure.com/login/canvas

Blaisure, K. R., Saathoff-Wells, T., Pereira, A., Wadsworth, S. M., & Dombro, A. L. (2016). *Serving military families, 2nd ed.* Routledge.

Center for Disease Control. (2021). Explosions and blast injuries A primer for clinicians.

Fyffe, D. C., Williams, J., Tobin, P., and Gibson-Gill, C. (2019). *Spinal cord injury veterans' disability benefits, outcomes, and health care utilization patterns: Protocol for a qualitative study.* JMIR Research Protocols. 8(10). e14039. https://doi.org/10.2196/14039

Kessler, R. A., Bhammar, A., Lakomkin, N., Shrivastava, R. K., Rasouli, J. J., Steinberger, J., Bederson, J., Hadjipanayis, C. J., & Benzil, D. L. (2021). Spinal cord injury in the United States Army Special Forces. *Journal of Neurosurgery: Spine.* 34, 110-116. https://doi.org/10.3171/2020.7.SPINE20804.

Mitchell, S. L., Hayda, R., Chen, A. T., Carlini, A. R., Ficke, J. R., & MacKenzie, E.J. (2019). The military extremity trauma amputation/limb salvage (METALS) study. *The Journal of Bone and Joint Surgery.* 101, 1470-1478. http://doi.org/10.2106/JBJS.18.00970

Morris, A. (2021, November 11). 'Dancing molecules' successfully repair severe spinal cord injuries. *Northwestern Now.* https://news.northwestern.edu/stories/2021/11/dancing-molecules-successfully-repair-severe-spinal-cord-injuries/

US Army Institute of Surgical Research. (2021). *Burn Center.* https://usaisr.amedd.army.mil/12_burncenter.html

US Department of Veterans Affairs. (2022). *Health issues related to service era.* https://www.va.gov/health-care/health-needs-conditions/health-issues-related-to-service-era/

US Department of Veterans Affairs Office of Research and Development. (2022a). *Hearing loss.* https://www.research.va.gov/topics/hearing.cfm

US Department of Veterans Affairs Office of Research and Development. (2022b). *Spinal cord injury.* https://www.research.va.gov/topics/sci.cfm

US Department of Veterans Affairs Office of Research and Development. (2022c). *Vision loss.* https://www.research.va.gov/topics/visionloss.cfm

Wallace, D. (2012). Trends in traumatic limb amputation in allied forces in Iraq and Afghanistan. *Journal of Military Veterans Health*, 20(2), 31-35.

Invisible Wounds
CHAPTER SIX

An invisible wound is a cognitive impairment, mental health condition, or behavioral condition arising from a traumatic event or a collection of adverse life events, typically associated with deployments (Tanielian & Jaycox, 2008). The phrase invisible wound first appeared in the 2008 RAND publication, *Invisible Wounds of War,* by Tanielian and Jaycox. This publication is considered the seminal study of these modern day wounds of war. It was at this same time that TBI was being termed a "signature wound," a new and profound injury that moved to the top of the charts in terms of frequency (Barnes, 2022). It was new and more frequent because of the improved protective battle armor and more timely medical care received by military personnel during battle. Military members were surviving more than in wars past and the use of IEDs were increasing the odds that a military member would sustain a TBI.

The most cited invisible wounds are PTSD, TBI, and Major Depressive Disorder (MDD). Two other conditions of note are General Anxiety Disorder (GAD) and Complicated Grief. First, PTSD is by far the most widely known, publicized, and often exploited invisible wound experienced by service members. Its effects can range from having minimal effect on daily life to being so debilitating that service members end up losing their jobs, families, homes, and their lives due to suicide. Second, TBI ranges from designations of mild to moderate to severe based on presenting conditions/symptoms. Mild TBI (mTBI), or concussions, can cause headaches, vision problems, and executive functioning problems. Although many mTBI clear up after several months, for some military members, mTBI can be a life-long debilitating condition. For moderate to severe TBI, the type of problems a person experiences typically depends on the area of the brain injury; therefore, understanding the neuroscience of invisible wounds is important. Rehabilitation can be long and service members may never achieve full functionality. Moreover, severe TBIs usually result in the need for full-time care. Repeated TBIs also pose a problem. Like repeated head injuries in sports (chronic traumatic encephalopathy or CTE), military members are at greater risk for other issues because of multiple TBIs. Behavioral changes can result in risky behavior, substance abuse, and trouble with the law. Oftentimes, members are discharged from the service for misbehavior; we now understand that these behavioral problems often stem from TBI. Finally, MDD is a condition often overlooked, but it is one of the most common invisible wounds. Because of the stigma of mental health conditions, many service members do not seek help for it. MDD is often a co-occurring condition with physical, moral, and other invisible (psychological) wounds.

Post-Traumatic Stress (PTS)

Post-traumatic stress can develop after a person has been directly exposed to, witnessed, or heard about a traumatic event, involving a threat of severe bodily harm or loss of life to themselves or others. Acute stress is the body's normal reaction to extremely abnormal events, but for some these symptoms do not remit. When symptoms of acute stress become prolonged, even after the threat is gone, and a person is diagnosed, the term post-traumatic stress disorder (PTSD) applies. Military personnel may be more at risk of exposure to traumatic events than the average civilian population due to their frequent deployments to combat zones.

Stress response (the concept of fight, flight, or freeze) is necessary for survival. Combat stress reaction ranges from healthy response and functioning to maladaptive responses. Exposure to prolonged, repeated stress drains individuals' stores of resiliency which can eventually have a negative effect on day-to-day functioning. Some of these maladaptive responses can manifest in the following ways: risky and dangerous behavior; thrill seeking; addiction to alcohol, drugs, gambling, and sex; and anger issues such as road rage (Blaisure et al., 2016).

The DoD strives to minimize combat stress reaction by implementing deployment/battle training, introducing stress and resiliency training, and establishing post-deployment assessment and debriefing. The goal of these programs is to better prepare military members for the psychological aspects of battle; build resiliency and provide strategies to cope with combat stress; and institute a decompression/debriefing period after deployment to assess the psychological health of service members and link them to available services.

At one time the VA National Center for PTSD outlined these symptoms of PTSD. While the original website page and this list are no longer available on their site, it is valuable information, nonetheless.

PTSD Symptoms

Re-experiencing Symptoms
- Frequent upsetting thoughts or memories of the traumatic event
- Recurring nightmares
- Acting or feeling as though the traumatic event were happening again (flashback)
- Having strong feelings of distress when reminded of the traumatic event
- Experiencing physical/physiological responses, such as racing heart or sweating, when reminded of the traumatic event

Avoidance Symptoms
- Making efforts to avoid thoughts, feelings, conversations about the traumatic event
- Making efforts to avoid places or people that remind you of the traumatic event

- Having difficulty remembering important parts of the event
- Loss of interest in important, positive activities
- Feeling distant from others
- Difficulty having positive feelings like happiness or love
- Feeling like your life may be cut short

Hyperarousal Symptoms
- Difficulty falling or staying asleep
- Feeling irritable, having angry outbursts
- Difficulty concentrating
- Constantly "on guard" or like danger is lurking around every corner
- Being jumpy or easily startled

Post-traumatic stress can affect every aspect of a military member's life—the ability to maintain healthy relationships, gain and maintain employment, and feel safe in his/her environment. It can also affect their willingness to seek help. Struggles with PTS/PTSD can lead to marital issues, family violence, substance abuse, financial and legal problems, homelessness and often suicide. It's important to note that family members often develop secondary trauma living with someone with PTS/PTSD.

Assessment and Treatment

Assessment of military PTSD is conducted with various tools and the use of the Diagnostic and Statistical Manual (DSM-V). The Post-traumatic Stress Checklist, PCL-5 assessment is one of the most common tools used to ascertain whether a person has PTSD. The self-test covers 20 symptoms covered in the DSM-V and is used for initial screening, initial diagnosis, and on-going treatment evaluation. Service members and veterans can take this self-test if they think they have PTSD. A copy of the assessment tool can be found at the VA Claims Insider website (https://vaclaimsinsider.com/va-ptsd-test/).

The DSM-V lists eight criteria, all of which must be met for a diagnosis of PTSD. Included in the list are a) exposure to a traumatic event, b) reexperiencing the event, c) avoiding trauma triggers, d) negative thoughts/feelings that got worse after the event, e) trauma related hyperarousal, f) symptoms last more than a month, g) symptoms cause functional distress or impairment, and h) symptoms are not caused by other factors.

Other diagnostic aids are the Clinician-Administered PTSD Scale (CAPS), a 30-item structured interview, which serves a similar purpose as the PCL-5; the PTSD Symptom Scale Interview (PSS-I-5), and the Post-traumatic Diagnostic Scale (PSD-5), which is another self-report assessment instrument. All the assessment tools listed in this section are based on the DSM-V, hence the -5 designation with each acronym. Additional information can be found at the VA PTSD website: https://www.ptsd.va.gov/professional/assessment/

Some of the traditional treatments for PTSD include cognitive therapy (cognitive processing therapy and cognitive behavioral therapy), prolonged exposure therapy, eye movement desensitization and reprocessing, stress inoculation therapy, and psychopharmacology. Transcranial Magnetic Stimulation (TMS) is also being used to treat PTSD along with other conditions such as major depression. An electromagnetic coil placed near the skull stimulates nerve cells in the brain which seems to alleviate symptoms of PTSD. Alternative approaches include veteran led groups and retreats, indigenous practices including sweat lodges, yoga therapy and meditation, Tai Chi, acupuncture, massage and bodywork therapies, Reiki, and ecotherapy.

Traumatic Brain Injury (TBI)

As mentioned in Chapter 5, Traumatic Brian Injury straddles the line between physical and invisible injuries. TBI is a physical injury; however, it has been dubbed an invisible injury since the injury cannot be seen by others. As such, others often don't understand the symptoms and results of the injury, especially when it is a mild or moderate brain injury.

There are two basic types of TBI—closed head injuries and penetrating injuries. Closed head injuries in the military are the result of blunt force trauma, falls, vehicle accidents, blast injuries, and sports injuries. The skull remains intact, and the damage is internal. Penetrating injuries happen when something passes through the skull and damages the brain tissue. This type of TBI in the military is usually the result of shrapnel, bullets, and contact with other objects after an explosion or fall.

TBI is one of the most prevalent battle injuries of recent times. TBIs are categorized based on diagnostic criteria of loss of consciousness (LOC) and the Glasgow Coma Scale, which assigns a numeric value to a person's response to directions to a) open eyes, b) give verbal response, and c) give a physical response. These results inform the characterization of the TBI—mild, moderate, and severe. The severity of the TBI has implications for the degree of service members' ability to carry out activities of daily living (ADL) and the degree to which they require care by others. Other diagnostic tools for assessing brain injury include imaging tests (x-rays, CT scans, and MRIs). These tests can help assess the damage in moderate to severe brain injury; however, mild TBIs often do not show any damage on these tests.

Types of TBI include a) contusions or bruises, b) hematomas (bleeds in the brain), c) skull fractures, d) diffuse axonal injuries (tears in the nerve fibers in the brain), and e) concussions that can result in loss of consciousness, memory, confusion, headaches, etc. (Johnson, 2010 as cited in Blaisure et al., 2016).

Mild TBI (mTBI) is the most frequently experienced TBI in the military. It is also the one that goes unreported and undetected most often. Most literature indicates mTBIs resolve on their own after several weeks or months; however, many service members experience lingering symptoms for years without resolution. Changes that result from TBI include

- Physical/neurological—headaches; balance and motor skill problems; vision, hearing, and language difficulties
- Cognitive—memory, executive functioning (planning and organizing, decision-making, concentration, self-regulation)
- Psychological—anxiety and depression, irritability, short-temper, emotional lability

- Behavioral—decreased inhibition, risky behavior, impulse control issues, lack of empathy (Fleming et al. n.d.)

These sequelae and recovery depend on factors such as
- Type of injury and how it occurred
- Severity of the injury and location on the brain
- Co-occurring conditions
- Individual and family response to injury
- Available treatments and resources

Traumatic brain injury affects the family as well as the service member. Dealing with even minor changes in cognitive, emotional, and behavioral function can be frustrating for family members. For moderate to severe TBI, the rehabilitation process and aftercare can take its toll on the family logistically, emotionally, and financially. Although the military and VA have instituted various programs to support service members, veterans, and families who deal with TBI, it is ultimately the family members who bear the responsibility for care.

Assessment and Treatment

As stated above, initial assessments are based on the Glasgow Coma Scale, LOC, and diagnostic imaging tests. These tests form the physical assessment of TBI. Other areas to assess include evaluating functional impairments (ability to carry out activities of daily living); cognitive impairments by evaluating concentration, short-term memory, problem solving, and executive functioning; and psychological effects by evaluating complaints of irritability, depression, anxiety, anger control, and low frustration tolerance impairment.

Treatment often includes rehabilitation, the length and nature of which depends upon the severity of the TBI. It can last a few months, years or even be present for a lifetime. Rehabilitation often involves physical, occupational, and speech therapy to help individuals relearn how to speak, read, walk, feed, and bathe themselves. Those with TBI, even mTBI, often need family assistance remembering things, transportation, money management, and understanding medical and other instructions. Behavioral changes and lack of impulse control can result in legal or disciplinary problems for service members and veterans. More severe injuries often mean the service member can no longer work and contribute to the household financially. Finally, in the most severe cases, service members/veterans may need 24-hour care.

Major Depressive Disorder (MDD)

Major Depressive Disorder (MDD) is often overshadowed by the other two invisible wounds of PTSD and TBI. It is also often paired with Generalized Anxiety Disorder (GAD). Many veterans will tell you that MDD and co-occurring issues are more prevalent; they just don't get the public attention. Perhaps it's because anyone can have these problems. Maybe it's because no one has attached "military" or "combat" to them. Whatever the reason, MDD just doesn't get press coverage until suicide happens. MDD can be just as elusive, just as debilitating as PTSD. When depression and anxiety flare up, they can be so inextricably entwined, it's hard to tell where one ends and the other begins.

MDD can occur alone or in conjunction with other invisible wounds or with other health issues such as physical injuries or substance abuse. Although PTSD gets top billing in the news and mental health circles, far more military members, and veterans report difficulties with depression due to persistent distress and impairment of daily functioning. Individuals with MDD do not experience the same symptoms, and the severity and duration of symptoms may vary.

Assessment and Treatment

Signs and Symptoms of Major Depression include:
- Persistent low mood
- Loss of interest in previously enjoyed activities
- Sleep problems
- Restlessness and agitation
- Feeling slowed down

- Concentration impairment
- Feelings of worthlessness
- Appetite disturbances
- Feeling hopeless or suicidal

MDD is assessed and diagnosed using DSM-V criteria and tools such as Patient Health Questionnaires, Beck Depression Inventory, and Major Depression Inventory, along with many others. Treatment for MDD typically involves psychotherapy and psychopharmacology elements, such as antidepressants. With the legalization of medical marijuana and the explosion of CBD shops around the country, these alternatives to pharmaceutical solutions have skyrocketed. Unfortunately, since there is still a strong stigma associated mental health issues and seeking help, many with MDD turn to alcohol and drugs to deal with their symptoms.

Generalized Anxiety Disorder (GAD)

Generalized Anxiety Disorder is characterized by long-lasting excessive worry and anxiety about life issues and day-to-day existence. People experiencing GAD often find it difficult to relax and have an inability to stop worrying even in the absence of major life stress. Normal anxiety and worry are considered an anxiety disorder when it is severe enough to interfere with normal life functioning such as social interaction or occupational performance. People experiencing an anxiety disorder often feel restless or on edge, have difficulty concentrating, are irritable, and experience sleep disturbances. Many military members, veterans, and families struggle with anxiety.

Assessment and Treatment

Assessment and treatment of GAD follows the same lines as those for MDD—a combination of medications and traditional therapy. Alternative approaches include some of the same modalities listed above for MDD. As mentioned earlier, MDD and GAD are often co-occurring disorders, so treatments often target both.

Complicated Grief

Complicated grief is not often mentioned in conversations about military mental health conditions, but it is important to highlight here. Delaney et al. (2017) describe complicated grief as "significant chronic impairment that stems from bereavement" (p. e1751). Complicated grief is long-lasting and so profound that its preoccupation takes over people's lives. Considering the loss many service members experience during deployments and the circumstances surrounding those losses, it's understandable that many may struggle with complicated grief. Compound these situations with elevated levels of stress, family separation, inability to make sense of the loss, and guilt pertaining to the loss, service members are at greater risk for developing complicated grief (Delaney, et al., 2017). Complicated grief can affect duty performance, physical health, family and social relationships, and lead to maladaptive behaviors such as substance abuse and suicide.

Signs and Symptoms of Complicated Grief
- Frequent yearning for and thoughts about the deceased
- Intense sorrow and pain over the loss
- Difficulty accepting the loss
- Bitterness or guilt about the loss
- Preoccupation with reminders of the deceased, or avoidance of these reminders
- Difficulty enjoying life or regaining a sense of purpose after the loss (Delaney, et al., 2017).

Assessment and Treatment
Identifying and diagnosing complicated grief can be done by using various assessment tools such as the Inventory for Complicated Grief or the Brief Grief Questionnaire. These tools help mental health professionals differentiate between typical grief and complicated grief. Complicated grief therapy combines cognitive behavioral therapy, motivational interviewing, and

psychoeducation to help the person move from a state of "stuckness" by learning to accept the loss and accompanying emotional pain and reach a point where the person can talk about the loss and circumstances surround it (Iglewicz, et al., 2020).

Secondary Trauma

Secondary trauma can develop in both social workers and military family members. Social workers can experience secondary trauma while working with military members who have been in battle or experienced other trauma such as sexual assault, so it's important to recognize the symptoms and what you and your organization can do to prevent or mitigate the effects of secondary trauma. Secondary trauma also often develops in military family members as a result of living with and/or caring for a service member/veteran who is suffering from trauma.

Secondary Trauma and the Mental Health Professional

Secondary trauma is all too common for professionals who provide health care, counseling, emergency care, and legal assistance to others. It is no different for the military community and those who serve military members and veterans. The fallout from working with traumatized populations ranges from job "burn-out" to full-blown displays of trauma symptoms, termed Secondary Traumatic Stress (Barnes, 2022). There are many articles available that address secondary trauma across various professional service sectors. In his article, *Mitigating Secondary Stress in Military Justice*, Wolrich (2019) identifies three mitigation strategies which typify the recommendations in many sources:

- Raising awareness about secondary stress/trauma among practitioners and leaders
- Creating a supportive environment by balancing caseloads, consulting supervisors, and seeking support of co-workers
- Practicing self-care

Secondary Trauma Among Family Members

Dealing with and caring for a military family member who has been traumatized by events on the battlefield or in the workplace (PTSD, military sexual trauma, etc.) can take its toll on family members. It's common for family members to develop similar symptoms as the trauma-affected military members. Treatment for secondary trauma is similar to the treatment for original trauma response.

Invisible or psychological wounds are just as prevalent as physical wounds in the military. Their invisibility often makes identification and treatment difficult. Moreover, the stigma of seeking mental health assistance prevents many service members and veterans from getting the help they need. These conditions can seriously affect the service member's ability to function daily and maintain healthy relationships. Additionally, failure to seek help can lead to maladaptive behaviors such as substance abuse, isolation, and avoidance of others. Post-traumatic stress, traumatic brain injury, major depressive disorder, and the lesser-known general anxiety disorder and complicated grief make up the constellation of invisible wounds. Finally, secondary trauma can emerge as the result of living with and working with service members who suffer from trauma. There are many assessment tools and treatments available for these conditions. There are many alternative treatment options emerging for service members and veterans that seek non-traditional remedies. Understanding the nature of these conditions and the treatment options available are necessary when working with the military population.

Final Thoughts

An invisible wound is a cognitive impairment, mental health condition, or behavioral condition arising from a traumatic event or a collection of adverse life events associated with military service, especially deployments. The three main invisible wounds are traumatic brain injury, post-traumatic stress disorder, and major depressive disorder. Two other conditions that often accompany physical and invisible injuries are general anxiety disorder and complicated grief. Family members and therapists can develop secondary trauma as a result of their interactions with the service member. Invisible wounds are difficult to recognize, diagnose, and understand by others because there are no outward physical wounds. These invisible wounds manifest in behavioral, emotional, and cognitive changes that often resemble other conditions. Interventions and new technology are constantly emerging, so it is important to review professional literature for both traditional and alternative approaches to treatment.

References

Barnes, S. D. (2022). *Invisible wounds* [Module overview]. Canvas. https://wnmu.instructure.com/login/canvas

Blaisure, K. R., Saathoff-Wells, T., Pereira, A., Wadsworth, S. M., & Dombro, A. L. (2016). *Serving military families, 2nd ed.* Routledge.

Delaney, E. M. Holloway, K. J., Miletich, D. M., Webb-Murphy, J. A., Lanouette, N. M. (2017). Screening for complicated grief in a military mental health clinic. *Military Medicine, 182,*(9/10), e1751-e1756.

Fleming, J., McVey, N., Shusterman, M., & DeHope, E. (n.d.). Brain injury: Important facts and implications for social work practice. *Social Work Today.* https://www.socialworktoday.com/archive/exc_070212.shtml

Iglewicz, A., Shear, M. K., Reynolds, C. F. III, Simon, N., Lebowitz, B., & Zisook, S. (2020). Complicated grief therapy for clinicians: An evidence-based protocol for mental health practice. *Depression and Anxiety. 37*(1), 90-98. https://doi.org/10.1002/da.22965

Tanielian, T., & Jaycox, L. H. (Eds.). (2008). *Invisible wounds of war: Psychological and cognitive injuries, their consequences, and services to assist recovery.* RAND Corporation.

US Department of Veteran Affairs. *National Center for PTSD.* (2023). https://www.ptsd.va.gov/

Wolrich, A. S. (2019). Mitigating secondary stress in military justice. *Army Lawyer,* 4, 44-47.

Moral Injury
CHAPTER SEVEN

Moral injury describes the spiritual damage or fallout resulting from witnessing or engaging in acts that are contrary to our moral/cultural/spiritual sense of self or code of ethics. This can result from a person's own decisions or actions or the actions and decisions of leaders or others. Moral injury results when actions or behaviors run counter to service members' ethical, moral, or religious foundations. It can be considered an assault on one's psychological and spiritual being, resulting in both short- and long-term effects ranging from feelings of guilt and shame to utterly impeding one's ability to function on a day-to-day basis. Moral injury manifests as guilt, shame, loss of faith or trust in authority and institutions, and/or disillusionment. Other signs include social isolation, lack of concern or empathy for others, loss of a spiritual connection, and loss of self-worth (Blaisure et al., 2016). Great strides have been made in researching and understanding what moral injury is and how it affects service members and families. Treatment approaches have also evolved to deal with moral injury.

Defining Moral Injury

Barnes et al. (2019) note that the original definition from research with Vietnam veterans focused solely on leadership failure and contained three criteria outlined by Shay (2002): "betrayal of what's right, by someone who holds legitimate authority, in a high stakes situation" (p. 99). Later definitions of moral injury shifted the focus to moral failings of the individual such as this one: "perpetuating or failing to prevent, bearing witness to or learning about acts that transgress deeply held moral beliefs and expectations" (Litz et al., 2009, p. 700). Frankfurt et al. (2018) describe moral injury as psychological harm from an event that runs counter to one's values. Originally defined within the context of acts of commission or omission, the definition was expanded to include non-combat situations, such as military sexual trauma. Yan (2016) further notes that moral injury is an existential concept regardless of religious or spiritual beliefs. Finally, researchers have yet to agree on an operational definition of moral injury, thus many research studies tie moral injury to PTSD, or choose to focus either on leadership responsibility or individual responsibility. By choosing one over the other, there is a failure to examine the effects of moral injury in its entirety. In essence, moral injury occurs when people experience an event that challenges or fractures their moral foundation. The event shakes their concept of right and wrong and causes them great grief or guilt along with other psycho-spiritual angst.

Moral Injury in the Context of Battle

Battle creates situations in which military members are confronted with moral and ethical choices. Their actions—resulting from their own decisions or the decisions of others—may contradict their moral beliefs and cause a crisis of faith or spirit. Military members in combat are exposed to all sorts of violence—death of teammates, recovery of the dead, civilian casualties—and all the associated sights, smells, and emotions. While these service members may be trained to kill, they may not be prepared to cope with the aftermath of combat. Additionally, unconventional warfare presents additional challenges as these actions often straddle the line of moral actions. Furthermore, extended and more frequent deployments creates an environment and mindset ripe for an increase in unethical behavior (Litz et al., 2009).

According to The Moral Injury Project, moral injury in the military arises from several sources:

- Using deadly force in combat and causing the harm or death of civilians, knowingly but without alternatives, or accidentally
- Giving orders in combat that result in the injury or death of a fellow service member
- Failing to provide medical aid to an injured civilian or service member
- Returning home from deployment and hearing of the executions of cooperating local nationals
- Failing to report knowledge of a sexual assault or rape committed against oneself, a fellow service member, or civilians
- Following orders that were illegal, immoral, and/or against the Rules of Engagement (ROE) or Geneva Convention
- A change in belief about the necessity or justification for war, during or after one's service (Syracuse University, 2022, para. 2)

Development and Effects of Moral Injury

Barnes et al. (2019) note that moral injury develops in response to a traumatic event that runs counter to a service member's moral code. In contrast to PTSD where the constellation of symptoms is associated with the emotions *at the time of the event*, symptoms of moral injury are associated with emotions that *arise after the event*. The extent to which it develops depends on the individual's interpretation of the traumatic event. Moral injury occurs when service members experience dissonance between what occurred and their moral code. If they are unable to make sense of or justify the act, moral injury will occur. It will not occur without the element of dissonance (Frankfurt et al., 2018; Litz et al., 2009).

These conflicts diminish self-image, and create guilt and shame or betrayal and anger, depending on the nature of the traumatic event (Frankfurt et al., 2018). Moral injury involving individual responsibility includes responses such as self-blame, trust issues and spiritual/existential conflict (Barnes et al., 2019). According to Sloan and Friedman (2008), guilt is often a by-product of deployment and battle ranging from the guilt of leaving family behind to survivor's guilt when a comrade is killed or injured. "Guilt results when people act against their moral values, doing things that are contrary to their beliefs" (p. 97). On the other hand, moral injury stemming from others' transgressions or responsibility can result in anger, trust issues, and a lack of forgiveness of others (Barnes et al., 2019).

Moral injury harms the human spirit, disabling individuals from a healthy life and goal attainment. It can be considered a spiritual struggle that causes a disconnect between the individual and others including higher spiritual powers. This struggle can also affect daily functioning in all realms—psychological, physical, social, spiritual. Brenault-Phillips et al. (2019) report that moral injury can result in psychological and behavioral problems—PTSD, sleep disturbance, intrusive thoughts, impulsive and self-harming behavior, substance abuse, social isolation, and suicide. Moral injury and the accompanying shame and guilt can lead to suicide ideation and suicide itself. This is especially true if the service member has killed (Blinka and Harris, 2016).

Sullivan & Starnino (2019) introduced the concept of damage to our assumptive world—the core beliefs that frame our world and provide stability and direction to our lives. Moral injury damages and challenges these beliefs and can result in an existential or spiritual crisis. Responses to moral injury include interpersonal problems (isolation, distrust), behavioral problems (acting out, domestic violence), and mental health challenges (depression, anxiety, substance abuse, suicide ideation). Like PTSD, it also can result in a state of "stuckness" that prevents a person from resolving the conflict and moving forward.

Moral Injury and Cognitive Dissonance

Moral injury always contains the element of cognitive dissonance. Cognitive dissonance, coined by Leon Festinger, is a psychological phenomenon which refers to the discomfort felt at a discrepancy between what you already know or believe, and new information or interpretation. As military members develop their battle mind, they learn a combat survival mentality that sometimes is in direct opposition to their original way of thinking. When forced to engage the battle mind and attendant battle responses, warriors are often faced with moral decisions. In the heat of battle, decisions are made in a split second; the processing of those decisions and their consequences after the event often lead to moral injury.

Treatment and Interventions

Effective treatments for moral injury are still being explored and developed. Current research and treatment approaches often attempt to target behaviors and psychological sequelae while putting the spiritual aspect of moral injury on the back burner. However, effective treatment necessitates including a focus on the connection to the spiritual aspects of the person's life. (Litz et al., 2009). Furthermore, evidence-based cognitive therapies have shown some success; however, the origins of moral injury—with their spiritual connection—require other considerations (Barnes et al., 2019). For example, since researchers often link PTSD and moral injury, it is assumed and often proposed that the same therapeutic approaches be used to treat moral injury. This is effective if military members/veterans have both conditions. However, applying cognitive or behavioral approaches to resolve moral injury is questionable. Attention must be paid to healing the spiritual body. Factors that foster positive outcomes and help the healing process include a) the ability to make meaning of the event and reconcile discrepancy between actions and belief system, and b) self-forgiveness and atoning for actions.

Treatments that have been found to be effective include adaptive disclosure, pastoral narrative disclosure, and combining mindfulness-based therapy with cognitive therapies (Barnes et al., 2019). Adaptive disclosure is a combat-specific, emotion-focused psychotherapy designed specifically for the Marine Corps. Pastoral narrative disclosure was designed for chaplains to use in their counseling sessions. This 8-step approach emphasizes telling the story and reflecting and reconstructing the traumatic event. Through the process military members and veterans can learn to reconnect with others and restore their moral bearings. Mindfulness techniques are the latest enhancement to many traditional interventions, teaching the concept of remaining present and attuned to the body and mind.

Litz et al. (2009) developed a treatment model to address moral injury. The model looks at the concepts of morals, moral beliefs, shame, and self-forgiveness and the risk factors of proneness to shame and neuroticism. It is a modified cognitive processing approach with seven features.

- Strong relationship with trusting, caring therapist
- Client education regarding the treatment process
- Short-term exposure-based framework of the event
- Examination of the event
- Imagined dialog with benevolent moral authority to help reframe or lend meaning to event
- Environment and process that fosters atonement and forgiveness
- Encouragement of social reconnection
- Plan for the future

The Role of Chaplains in Treating Moral Injury

Chaplains in military service have served a time-honored and vital role since the beginning of war. They go to war with only their faith to protect them. They do not carry weapons. In the last few decades, the US military chaplaincy has expanded to include chaplains from all faiths which speaks volumes about how the US Military views the importance of faith in the life of a warrior.

Chaplains provide all the typical services you might think of in a house of worship: leading services, conducting spiritual rites/rituals, and providing spiritual counsel. One of the most noteworthy features of military chaplaincy is the strict adherence to confidentiality. This is a compelling reason military members seek out chaplain counseling services. Chaplains can play a vital role in treating moral injury.

Moral dilemmas occur when military actions conflict with spiritual or religious beliefs. The complex intertwining of mental, emotional, and spiritual reactions to battle must be addressed if complete healing is to happen. The heat of battle requires quick response, and these actions often conflict with the warrior's moral foundation. Warriors do not have time to process the decision and the consequences until after the event. A chaplain embedded in a combat unit can help unit members process moral dilemmas and minimize moral injury (Barnes, 2022). Moral injury tests our religious and spiritual beliefs. Sloan and Friedman (2008) note that a warrior's faith may be strengthened or decimated on the battlefield. Battle can cause warriors to question their faith and belief system. Anger, guilt, disillusionment can consume the warriors to the point where it is detrimental to daily functioning and interpersonal relationships. Once a warrior returns from battle, counseling with a chaplain can help a warrior continue to heal the moral injury. Confidentiality during chaplain counseling sessions is protected; often warriors will meet with chaplains rather than mental health counselors because of this protection. Furthermore, many VA clinics and veterans' centers have chaplains on hand for counseling.

Social Work Intervention

It is essential that social workers be competent and comfortable providing treatment that incorporates and addresses the spiritual aspect of moral injury, as spirituality comprises the main element. Yan (2016) suggests that although social workers may feel competent and capable of applying evidence-based treatments in a therapeutic setting, they often feel ill-equipped or reluctant to address the spiritual aspects of veterans' issues during treatment. If social workers do not feel confident to address moral injury, they can enlist the help of chaplains or clergy to create a holistic therapeutic approach. Blinka and Harris (2016) believe chaplains and social workers can work together to treat moral injury. Additionally, they note that areas of professional competency include a) therapeutic presence and unconditional understanding; b) proper application of trauma treatment modalities; c) integration of faith and practice; and d) use of assessment and intervention techniques applicable to moral injury. Finally, Sullivan and Starnino (2019) assert that understanding and helping veterans with moral injury and the attendant spiritual challenges is part of multi-cultural competency.

Indigenous Healing Practices

Indigenous healing practices are those found in original cultures of a nation: First Peoples, Native American, Eskimo/Inuit, Pacific Islander, and Hispanic indigenous cultures. Information about the healing practices of Indigenous Peoples of North America are seldom found on websites. If you want help from a Shaman, Curandero/a, Native American Spiritual Healer, or Inuit Shaman (Angakos), oftentimes you must either belong to that tribe or be willing to travel to the healer. Their practices are sacred, so they are not often shared outside their own communities. Yet some practices are being shared with those outside the specific group. For example, you can learn about the indigenous healing practices of Guam's CHamoru (Native Guam) healer, or *suruhanu* from a few websites such as https://micronesica.org/sites/default/files/mcmakin-2mincomb.pdf and https://www.guampedia.com/ancient-chamorro-medicine-making/. Finally, First Nation/Native Americans have been serving in the military since WWI. Ceremonies for the return, reintegration, and healing of warriors have existed since their tribes' inception. Sacred healing practices for veterans are now available to other veterans outside tribal boundaries. The sweat lodge and ceremony is one of the most well-known Indigenous healing practices. Below is a website that tells you about a sweat lodge for veterans. http://www.vasweatlodge.org/

Although moral injury is not classified as an invisible injury, it fits. It leaves no visible scars but does result in psychological and behavioral manifestations that can have a profound effect on a person's daily functioning. Researchers who lump moral injury and PTS together and propose the same treatments for both present a disservice to veterans and military members. Treating the spirit with mind therapies is partial treatment. Practitioners must be willing to combine psychological and spiritual approaches to facilitate healing. Chaplains and other spiritual advisors can fill a vital role in supporting and working with social workers who counsel those with moral injury.

Final Thoughts

The definition of moral injury has changed over the years depending upon the interests and focus of research. Originally defined as the result of failed leadership resulting in a sense of betrayal and anger, it now focuses on individual responsibility resulting in shame or guilt. While researchers may choose one angle or the other, for therapeutic interventions to be effective, we must consider both aspects. Moral injury develops out of a conflict with a person's moral code. It is different from PTS--PTS symptoms are associated with the emotions *at the time of the event*, symptoms of moral injury are associated with emotions that *arise after the event*.

It is essential that mental health professionals be competent and comfortable providing treatment that incorporates and addresses the spiritual aspect of moral injury, as spirituality comprises the main element. Chaplains and clergy are equipped to handle spiritual aspect of therapy: mental health professionals can enlist their advice and cooperation in treating moral injury. Therapeutic interventions must include a spiritual aspect to them if treatment is to be effective. We can learn from Indigenous healers. Indigenous healing practices address the mind, body, and spirit. There is no separation between them. Shamans from these cultural groups are uniquely qualified to address moral injury and the healing of the damaged spirit. Some of these practices are beginning to be shared with the greater population, such as sweat lodges specifically geared toward military members and veterans.

References

Barnes, H. A., Hurley, R. A., & Taber, K. H. (2019). Moral injury and PTSD: Often co-occurring yet mechanistically different. *Journal of Neuropsychiatry and Clinical Neuroscience, 31*(2), 98-103.

Barnes, S. D. (2022). *Moral wounds and spiritual healing* [Module overview]. Canvas. https://wnmu.instructure.com/login/canvas

Blaisure, K. R., Saathoff-Wells, T., Pereira, A., Wadsworth, S. M., & Dombro, A. L. (2016). *Serving military families, 2nd ed.* Routledge.

Blinka, D., & Harris, H. W. (2016). Moral injury in warriors and veterans: The challenge to social work. *Social Work & Christianity, 43*(3), 7–27.

Brenault-Phillips, S., Pike, A., Scarcella, F., & Cherwick, T. (2019). Spirituality and moral injury among military: A mini-review. *Frontiers in Psychiatry, 10.* https://doi.org/10.3389/fpsyt.2019.00276

Frankfurt, S. B., DeBeer, B. B., Morissette, S. B., Kimbrel, N. A. LaBash, H., & Meyer, E. C. (2018). Mechanisms of moral injury following military sexual trauma and combat in post 9/11 US war veterans. *Frontiers in Psychiatry, 9.* https://doi.org/10.3389/fpsyt.2018.00520

Litz, B. T., Stein, N., Delaney, E., Lebowitz L., Nash, W. P., Silva, C., & Maguen, S. (2009). Moral injury and moral repair: A preliminary model and intervention strategy. *Clinical Psychology Review, 29,* 695-706. https://doi.org/10.1016/j.cpr.2009.07.003

Shay. J. (2002). *Odysseus in America: Combat trauma and the trials of coming home.* Scribner.

Sloan & Friedman. (2008) *After the war zone: A practical guide for returning troops and their families.* Da Capo Press.

Sullivan, W. P., & Starnino, V. R. (2019). Staring into the abyss: Veterans' accounts of moral injuries and spiritual challenges. *Mental Health, Religion, & Culture, 22*(1), 25-40. https://doi.org/10.1080/13674676.2019.1578952

Syracuse University. (2022). *The moral injury project.* https://moralinjuryproject.syr.edu/about-moral-injury/

Yan, G. W. (2016). The invisible wound: Moral injury and is impact on the health of operation enduring freedom/operation Iraqi freedom veterans. *Military Medicine, 181,* 451-457. https://doi.org/10.7205/MILMED-D-15-00103

Family Stress and Resilience
CHAPTER EIGHT

Families face changes and stressful situations from multiple sources: day-to-day living, shifting roles and diversity in family structure, economic fluctuations, accidents and illness, natural disasters, civil unrest, and wars. Once a safe zone for its members, the family is now stretched thin to meet the demands of daily living. When these changes and demands become greater than the family's capability to muster the resources needed to deal with them, disruption to the family system and functioning occurs.

The demands of daily military life, including deployments to battle zones, increase the stress on service members and their families. These unique characteristics of military life--frequent deployments, separations, and relocations—have a continuous and cumulative effect on military families. Further compounding the matter are the physical, psychological, and moral injuries many service members incur. Military life not only affects the service member but tends to have a profound influence on the family members' ability to navigate various aspects of military life. Response to military life encompasses both behavioral and psychological realms.

Previous chapters detailed aspects of military life and many of the challenges service members and their families encounter. Living away from extended family, marrying young, frequent moves and separations, spouse education and employment hurdles, the risk of deployments to dangerous locations, and finally separation from the military, all converge to make military life stressful. Theories and models about how families deal with stressors are the focus of this chapter.

Stress Theories and Models

Over the years, many theories, models, and ideas have evolved around stress and resiliency that guide social workers. In this chapter we explore some of these theories. The effect of stress on the family caregiver is great, so we apply the stress process model to the caregiving situation as well.

Studies of family stress began in the early 20th century as the world became more industrialized, urbanized, and less personalized. Throughout this time, geographic mobility, economic depressions and recessions, wars, and rapid technological advances have challenged the family's ability to manage and respond to life's stressors (Bush et al., 2017). Early family stress theories seem to begin with Rubin Hill in the 1940s followed by the works of Hans Selye, Hamilton McCubbin and Joan Patterson, Leonard Pearlin, Pauline Boss, and Froma Walsh among others. Resiliency theories and models grew out of early theories about stress and the capacity to deal with stressful events. Theories and models of stress and resilience help practitioners understand the concept of resilience, how to assess challenges that individuals and families face, and identify individual and collective strengths. A theoretical framework also helps us conduct research to develop the most effective prevention and treatment approaches. We can look at stress theories from an individual perspective and a systems perspective. Hans Selye is one of the early researchers of the individual response to stress.

Stress and Stressors

Stress and stressors are the key elements of the theories and models presented in this chapter, so a quick explanation is in order. Stress is the condition (physiological, emotional, etc. response) that arises when faced with situations (stressors) that challenge our state of being and functioning. The concept of stress follows a continuum ranging from challenges of everyday living to responses to traumatic events. Individual stress is seen as a process and a state of being. As a process, the focus is on the interaction of a person in his/her environment and the cognitive and behavioral responses resulting from appraising the stressful situation. When there is a mismatch between perception of the situation and the ability to meet the demands of the situation, a state of being stressed ensues. Family stress occurs when the equilibrium of a family system is disrupted causing the family to act to regain balance.

A stressor is an event, condition, or situation—real or imagined—that stimulates the stress response in an individual. The response is in the form of physiological and psychological reactions that affect the mind and body. These can be seen as threats to safety and security, stemming from the mind or external environment. There are two types of stressors: typical or normative and unexpected or non-normative. Change and transition (marriages, promotions, moves) are considered normative stressors of military life; non-normative stressors would be short-notice assignments or deployments, injury, or death resulting from military service.

General Adaption Syndrome

We can start with the work of Hans Selye who first identified stress as a physiological response process in his General Adaption Syndrome Model in 1956. The model highlights how an individual's state of homeostasis or equilibrium is affected by stress and the three stages involved in the pattern of responses to that stressor. The stages include alarm, resistance, and exhaustion. The alarm stage is when a threat is perceived which elicits the fight, flight, or freeze response. The resistance stage involves the time and resources required to offset or fend off the stress. If the stress persists and resources are depleted, the final stage ensues—exhaustion. This state can affect the mental and physical health (depression, heart conditions, immune system ailments, etc.) of the individual if the stress cannot be ameliorated. In 1983, Selye added that the stress response was contingent on the person's perspective. The outcome could be positive or negative based on how the experience and attendant symptoms were interpreted.

Systems and Ecological Frameworks

Family stress theories stem from a system-based or ecological framework. Families are viewed as an individual system of members and as a subsystem within a greater community system. Family stress theory focuses on the family unit and the interaction between its members and interaction with the outside world. The ecological framework allows us to evaluate the family in the context of a larger social environment. How families respond to stress depends on the interaction of the family with the larger community (Bush et al., 2017). Furthermore, psychobiological stress models look at how person's physiological, biological, social, and psychological systems interact and respond to stress while conservation of resources theories explain how people locate, amass, and protect resources that help them cope with stress.

In any living system, the primary goal is to maintain homeostasis or equilibrium between interdependent elements. In a family, the goal is to maintain healthy functioning and relationships among all members. This equilibrium/homeostasis is jeopardized when the family is faced with adversity or stressful situations. From a family systems perspective, family stress is defined as a disruption of the family system requiring adjustment or adaptation. Stress affects each member of the family system differently. Furthermore, each family member contributes differently and to different extents to restore family equilibrium. Stress and stressors--events and circumstances that contribute to or influence healthy family functioning--are integral components in understanding resilience. The stress response process, its concepts, and their relationship, begins with Hill's ABC-X Model.

ABC-X Model (1949/1958)

The ABC-X and Double ABC-X models form the basis of family resilience theory and other models. The ABC-X Model was developed by Rubin Hill in 1949 and refined in 1958. In this model, we consider variables in the pre-crisis stage: the nature of the precipitating stressful event (stressor event), family resources, and perception or meaning attached to the stressful event. The interaction of these three variables will determine the degree to which the event creates a challenge or a crisis. This outcome can be considered along a continuum—minor disruption to crisis.

$$A + B + C = X$$

Variable A = Precipitating stressful event. It is a situation for which the family had little or no preparation and is perceived as a problem. (an unexpected (non-normative) event as opposed to a normative or expected event such as marriage or graduation). The stressful event is viewed as something different that changes the routine functioning within the family. The degree to which the response to the event results in stress depends on the enormity of the event, whether it is a singular event or one of a collection of stressful events. Another consideration is the hardships the family sees that accompany the stressful event and how they might tax family resources.

Variable B = Family resources for facing the stressful event. The ability to secure and use appropriate resources to deal with stress influences the level of disruption in the family. Resources include both internal and external supports. Internal resources are internal traits/characteristics of family members and relationship among family members and ability to work together. External supports include available community/social supports such as extended family, friends, organizations, and institutions (Bush et al., 2017). Family resources are considered protective factors if they exist, and the family uses them to cope with stressful event. They are risk factors if the family has little to no resources to deal with stressful event. Their absence will lead to a crisis (X).

Variable C = This variable pertains to how the family defines (interprets/assigns meaning) the stressful event and the attendant hardships. If the family views the stressor as crisis-producing rather than challenging, the family would be more prone to experience a crisis. Belief systems and locus of control are considerations. Does the family see the situation as one they have a sense of mastery or control over (internal locus of control) or do they view themselves as having no control over the situation (external locus of control, fatalistic beliefs)? Protective factors relate to shared family beliefs and perceptions of the stressor and a positive and constructive outcome. The meaning that the family assigns to the event becomes a risk factor if the family looks upon the stressful event as a negative thing that will be difficult to cope with.

X = The stress or crisis is the interplay of the event, the resources available and used, and how the family defines the event. Stress is a change in family equilibrium, deemed positive or negative, and is considered a continuous variable that presents challenges of some sort daily. Families that have and use resources or know how to access resources and view the event as a stressful challenge can reestablish equilibrium. Crises, on the other hand, represent an either-or condition; the situation either creates a crisis or it does not. If the family does not have or use available resources or perceives the event as insurmountable, the family will experience a crisis.

Double ABC-X model (1983)

McCubbin and Patterson expanded Hill's ABC-X model with several elements including post-crisis variables to further forecast a family's capacity to deal with stressful events. Additional factors include a) additional life stressors and strains; b) psychological, intrafamilial, and social resources; c) changes in the family's definition; d) family coping strategies; and e) outcomes. Family coping strategies play a major role in this model. The model has three main parts: pre-crisis, crisis, and post-crisis (Meadows et al., 2016).

The pre-crisis stage contains Hill's ABC elements that lead to a crisis (X. The post-crisis stage includes an accumulation (pile up) of other stressors on top of the original event such as continuing hardships from the original stressor (Aa); new and existing resources (Bb); and the perception of these combined stressors and resources (Cc). The cumulative variables create a state of adaptation, either poorly- or well- adapted (Meadows et al., 2016). This model represents the movement of the family through time, whereas the ABC-X model represents a single event in time.

Family Adjustment and Adaptation Response (FAAR) Model

The FAAR Model elaborates on the Double ABCx model developed by McCubbin and Patterson by explaining the process by which a family adjusts and adapts to situations. Family adjustment and adaptation are contingent on how members balance demands with the strategies and processes they used to meet those demands. Crises occur when the demands outweigh the capabilities of the family. Protective factors, life cycle stages, and family rituals are identified as elements that can guide practitioners in understanding family resilience. Other key concepts include self-reliance, connection to others in the same situation, and self-assessment and perception of their capability to cope (Meadows et al., 2016).

Coping Theory

Coping is another concept related to stress and resilience. Coping consists of actions and strategies employed to overcome or adapt to stressful situations. It is the result of appraising a situation and selecting cognitive and behavioral actions that will help deal with the event. Coping is the process of applying internal resources to environmental demands. It is a fluid, dynamic response to the situation. Coping can be problem-focused or emotion-focused. Problem-solving approaches involve establishing specific goals to resolve the issue. Emotion-focused coping using strategies to alter the personal meaning of relationships or the event and making new meaning out of the event.

Conservation of Resources Theory/Model

Conservation of Resource theory posits that people strive to attain, build, protect, conserve, and use valued resources to cope with stressful situations and events. Threats to these resources, such as the perception of loss or actual loss of resources or when the efforts to obtain resources outweigh the gain, create stress (Hobfoll, 1989). This theory holds a systems or ecological perspective in that it views the individual within the context of family which is immersed in the community.

Resources are objects, personal characteristics, conditions, or energies that are valued by the person or are a means to securing these resources. Social supports, while not identified as a specific resource, play a role in facilitating the acquisition and preservation of resources. During a stressful event/situation, individuals will employ their resources to cope with the event/situation. When individuals and families have an adequate supply of resources and know how to use them, they effectively cope with the situation. However, if their resource supply is limited or has been taxed through a series of events, individuals and families may find themselves in crisis. Additionally, if an individual or family expends more energy and other resources to replace a lost resource, they may experience a loss of confidence in their ability to meet future demands. During times of no stress, people will work toward shoring up their resources to prepare for future stressful events. The ability to secure and save resources enhances confidence in the ability to cope with stressful times. This assessment or appraisal is an essential element in conservation of resource theory and ties in with stress appraisal theory developed by Lazarus and Folkman (Hobfoll, 1989; Hobfoll et al., 2008). Finally, individuals and families that hold a positive worldview and confidence in their ability to secure and use them tend to navigate through situations better than others. Along this same line, the ability to change how resources are valued when faced with their loss can minimize the stress that results from that lost resource. The conservation of resources model can help us understand how individuals obtain, save, and use valued resources to cope.

Stress Process Model

The Stress Process Model is attributed to Leonard Pearlin who spent decades researching the effects of stress and the processes involved in dealing with stressors in our lives. Like Hill's ABC-X model, the main elements of the stress process model include the source of the stress, the mediating resources, and the outcomes or manifestations of stress. Stress can arise from two sources: a specific event (eventful experience) and a buildup of continuous stress over time (life strains). Organisms, including people, operate best in a state of equilibrium or homeostasis. When change happens, the organism will work to regain this homeostasis. The activities involved in regaining balance can be tiring work and thus stressful. Change is inevitable throughout our lives, how we deal with those changes—whether a specific event, or compilation of life strains—determines the effect stress will have on us and those around us (Bush et al., 2017). Additionally, Pearlin et al. (1981) suggest that stress can affect our self-concept, our sense of mastery, and self-esteem. Stressful situations challenge our notion of how well we think we can and do handle events, our sense of control and mastery of the situation. Specific events can lead to a long-term strain on families. If we feel as though we are not successful in navigating through these continuous strains, it can erode our self-esteem and self-worth.

Many of the injuries presented earlier—physical injuries, PTSD, TBI, SCI—involve some level of care by family members. Caring for a wounded service member is stressful and exhausting. Matthieu and Swensen (2013) discuss Pearlin's caregiver stress process model and apply it to military family caregivers. The first step is examining the background and context of stress involved by getting a complete picture of what the caregiver is going through. Understanding the context of stressor is important for the family and the social worker. Boss (2001) suggests considering the source of the stressor, type of stressor, anticipated duration of stressor, and what other stressors are present. Second, a history of the injury and health of the service member and the length of time care has been provided adds to the understanding. A third area is the nature and duration of the relationship between the injured member and the caregiver. The second step is to consider the mediators. Mediators include factors that can change the trajectory of the path to minimize the stress and move in a more positive direction. Availability of resources, employing coping strategies, and building social support contribute to reducing stress (Matthieu & Swensen, 2013). Knowing what resources are available and accessible to the family and caregiver is essential as well. To help manage and deal with stress, we employ mediating resources. Two main resource mediators are social support and coping. The ability to secure and utilize social support has an effect on the outcome of situations. Coping or employing strategies to help us adjust or adapt to situations comes in three forms: modifying the situation that is causing the stress, modifying the meaning of the situation, and managing the stress using various tactics (Bush et al., 2017). Lastly, the outcomes represent the combined effect of the stressors on the caregiver and family.

So how do we integrate these theories into an effective helping strategy for the caregiver? We do this by investigating and evaluating each area areas. As with any case, we delve into the background and identify all pertinent information. In this instance, we look at the caregiver--our primary focus--and his/her current care-giving situation. We also get information about the wounded service member, his/her experience, healing process, level of self-care, etc. We also look at the relationship between the two. Was it a strong, healthy relationship prior to the service member's injury? Is it a strong, healthy relationship now? How has the relationship changed? How does each person feel about the role changes? Lastly, we look at the extent of care that is being provided and the access to services in the community. Are there community resources? Is the caregiver using them? If not, why? This extensive background review provides us a foundation for evaluating the existing stressors, the mediators of those stressors (coping strategies and social supports), and the outcomes/manifestations of the stress--the effects on the caregiver's mental, physical, emotional, spiritual health. When we examine/identify the caregiver's response to stress and its effects on the caregiver, we can select the best place to focus our attention: the environment of the stressful event, the caregiver's physical or cognitive response, or the strategies they use to cope with the event (Mattieu & Swensen, 2013, p.413). Understanding how the stress process model works guides us in developing psychoeducational materials and programs and interventions to help families to deal with stressful events.

Matthieu and Swensen (2013) incorporate the appraisal process into the assessment phase. Here the social worker looks at how the caregiver perceives the magnitude of the situation and his/her ability to handle the situation. The social worker has two options: a) help the caregiver objectively assess the situation and b) help the caregiver objectively assess the ability to deal with the situation. When caregivers are overwhelmed, they often cannot see things clearly. The social worker can help them do so. The concept of coping can also help the social worker. We all cope with situations differently, sometimes with healthy and appropriate responses, sometimes in unhealthy ways. The social worker looks at how the caregiver is coping and helps with problem-solving coping by engaging in strategies that lead to a resolution or change in the situation. This is done through problem-solving and decision-making tactics. The social worker can also help with emotion-focused coping by helping the caregiver change the way they feel or think about the situation. Oftentimes, re-framing the situation—seeing it differently, assigning new meaning, etc.—can relieve stress associated with the situation.

Resilience

The terms resilience and resiliency are well-worn words in today's vocabulary. We have resilient individuals, teams, ethnic and racial groups. We hear about the resiliency of people facing disaster, hardship, and personal tragedy. It is also the focus of concern and intervention within the military community. In this section we review definitions of resilience, look at Walsh's system theory of family resilience, consider the relationship of military readiness to resilience, and take a quick peek at assessment and treatment considerations.

Defining Resilience

The first step to understanding concepts of individual and family resilience is to define resilience and explore the context in which it is examined. Definitions have changed over time, depending on the focus of the research. Initially, resilience was studied as an individual trait, so definitions revolved around that notion. Eventually, the focus turned to a systems perspective—how the individual operated within the environment to develop resilience. Finally, the concept of family resilience emerged, focusing on both the individual in the family as well as the family as a unit. Within the military context, strengthening resilience emerged as a two-pronged approach focusing on the individual as well as the family. Resilience is often linked to the concept of military readiness. While there are initiatives to develop individual resilience in the military branches, strengthening family resilience and hence readiness, is the primary objective of military family programs. Finally, resilience is also conceptualized as both an outcome and as a process. Let's look at some definitions.

Definitions of resilience contain similar elements and key words. Two general definitions are from the Defense Center of Excellence and Institute of Medicine (DCEIM) and Blaisure et al. (2016). The DCEIM defines resilience as "the ability to withstand, recover, and grow in the face of stressors and changing demands" (Meadows et al., 2018, p. 2). Blaisure et al. (2016) incorporate similar elements in their definition: a "process of positive adaptation and growth after experiencing an adverse event or circumstance" (pp. 104-105). These definitions suggest resilience is a process that calls upon individual capacity and resourcefulness. Meadows et al. (2016) include in their definition a positive response to adversity and growth because of traumatic experience. Positive response leads to a family being able to find and use resources, and confidence in its ability to face adversity in the future. It also implies a stronger family functioning (teamwork) after the event. Simply put, resilience pertains to how well a person or family can bounce back, recover, adjust, or adapt to adverse situations and events.

Resilience as a process includes risk and protective factors that influence the outcome or response to stressful or traumatic events. According to van Breda (2018) the resilience process or protective factors are what help people achieve positive outcomes. Some of these include the

- importance of relationships, especially those that are nurturing and caregiving

- interaction with social support systems that include family, schools, religious institutions, neighborhoods, friends, and associates (person-in-environment concept)
- interplay of neurobiological factors such as genetics, developmental factors, brain development, and environmental conditions.

There is a process of engaging in activities or an interaction of conditions/factors leading to an outcome housed in a systems-based framework.

Resilience as a State or Outcome vs Process

Deciding whether to treat resilience as a state/outcome or a process is important in researching the phenomenon of resilience. Van Breda (2018) emphasized the importance of an operational definition of resilience in developing a theoretical framework. To conceptualize van Breda's model of resilience as an outcome or a process, he proposes that two different terms be used for the model. Resilience is best used with process definitions and resilient is best used for outcome definitions. For example, individuals are **resilient** when they achieve positive outcomes from adverse events and the **resilience** of a person comes from factors such nurturing support systems and a positive outlook. Van Breda (2018) offers this definition of resilience: "The multilevel processes that systems engage in to obtain better-than-expected outcomes in the face or wake of adversity" (p. 4). The term multilevel processes implies a systems approach; we do not operate alone; we are part of other systems that can influence and support us when dealing with adverse conditions.

Theoretical perspectives and their attendant definitions changed over the decades. Resilience can be defined on an individual level or may encompass a holistic view using a systems approach. It can also refer to the "competencies or capacities of people, while others refer to it as positive functioning in the face of adversity" (van Breda, 2018, p. 2). Resilience theories came from studies of adversity and its negative effect on people; hence resilience was often tied to dysfunction or a breakdown in a person's wellbeing. Studies were outcome-focused and typically focused on the mental health aspect of coping with adversity (van Breda, 2018).

Why do some people fare well in the face of adversity while others become overwhelmed? What traits and conditions determine how well a person will respond to adverse situations? Outcome oriented definitions of resilience include a path of healthy functioning, positive outcomes, unexpected outcomes after experiencing an adverse event. These outcome definitions focus on resilience as a state of being. Asking the question, "Why do some people fare well while others seem to become overwhelmed when faced with adversity?" shifts the focus of research from outcome to process. What other factors or processes influence (mediate) outcomes? To gain a comprehensive understanding of resilience, theories and research need to include three components: adversity (the precipitating event), process (mediating factors and processes), and outcome. Focusing on the process helps researchers explain the outcomes that ensue from an adverse event. It is this perspective that is most beneficial to social workers and those who develop effective interventions.

Individual and Family Resilience

The study of resilience began with a focus on individual traits and grew to include a systems view, taking into consideration individuals in their group environments (families, communities, etc.). Definitions of individual resilience include elements of being able to recover from adversity. This assumes that stress results in negative outcomes and requires coping behaviors. Individual resilience definitions often include the concept of hardiness—a character trait that helps individuals weather stressful times. Other elements pertaining to individual resilience include the ability to address the circumstance, making meaning of the event, and how the event is perceived and interpreted (Meadows et al., 2016).

When examining family resilience researchers found that this concept is more than the sum of its parts, a natural conclusion from a systems perspective. Meadows et al., (2016) researched family resilience within the DoD and noted that definitions stemmed from two perspectives, an individual's resilience within the family and family resilience as a unit. Today's models and theoretical perspectives highlight families as a unit and suggest a family's collective resilience is much greater than the capability of each family member. This is not to say that individual contributions are not important. On the contrary, Simon et al (2005) note that positive adult influences include a strong sense of spirituality, acceptance of others, positive outlook, sense of purpose, and the ability to flex with changing situations. Confidence in the family's ability to navigate trouble waters is also a key element. Children's contributions are assessed relative to their developmental level. Furthermore, family resilience definitions include common elements of a) the family exhibiting a positive response to adverse events or situations and b) the family experiencing growth in their confidence, resourcefulness, and perception as a strong unit. Finally, constructs in family resilience models include challenge vs crisis; developmental life stage; available support; and the concepts of adaptation, adjustment, and coping (Simon et al., 2005).

Systems Theory of Family Resilience

Stressors affect families and their response and resourcefulness to those stressors determine the outcome for family members and family as a unit. MacDermid et al. (2008) identified characteristics of resilience. Resilience is a dynamic process that develops over time. It is strength-based and situation specific. Resilience is strengthened in many ways and jeopardized when multiple risk factors are present.

Family resilience models and frameworks posit that traumatic and adverse events reverberate throughout the family system and that specific family processes influence their response to these events. Strengths-based interventions look at the various factors that mitigate a family's vulnerability to stress, support healing and growth, and empower families to face adversity. Additionally, this framework helps explain why resilient families do not develop psychological conditions from trauma or adversity.

Early theories looked at the family as a risk factor rather than a source of resilience and interventions focused on treating problems and deficits of families (Walsh, 2003). A change in perspective resulted in a conceptualization of resilience that contained elements of risk and protective factors/processes and individual, family, and sociocultural influences. Walsh, a prominent researcher in the field of family resilience developed interventions that highlighted strengths and resources of families and members. Walsh's concept of resilience centers around "understanding healthy family functioning in situations of adversity" and the ability to "grow and recover from those experiences" (p.1). Moreover, Walsh believes resilience is strengthened through caring relationships that nurture its members further supporting the systems and family perspective.

Walsh's family resilience framework looks at the family as a unit, a system. Crises and chronic stressors affect the entire family and its functioning as a system. Beyond simply coping and managing stressful events, family resilience theory involves a family's potential for transformation and growth. Out of adversity can come renewed and strengthened relationships, a shift in priorities, and new perspectives and abilities. Family crises often result from a series of stressful events that build up and jeopardize a family's ability to cope. It strains family functioning and the processes and strategies they normally use to combat adversity (Walsh, 2003). Walsh's model consists of three essential processes that can either foster or impede resilience.

Family Processes that Foster or Impede Resilience
Walsh (2003, 2012) identifies and describes three main processes that are used by families to address stressful events in their lives. How these processes are employed and qualified (well-functioning or broken) can mean the difference between successfully navigating the stressful situation or the situation becoming a crisis. The three processes are family belief systems, organizational patterns, and communication and problem solving. Family belief systems include making meaning of adversity, having a positive outlook, and transcendence and spirituality. Organizational patterns used by a family include flexibility, connectedness, social and economic resources. The third process is

communication and problem solving which involve clear, consistent messages, open emotional expression, collaborative problem solving.

Family Belief Systems. When a crisis occurs, the well-functioning family faces the adverse event as a team. Their ability to assign meaning and face the challenge with a positive outlook enhances their ability to navigate and grow through the experience. Additionally, having a spiritual framework or connection within which to deal with adversity also fosters a positive outcome. Spiritual rituals and resources, and the practice of prayer and meditation also foster healthy coping. The concept of transcendence or ability to move beyond a situation involves emerging from the situation with transformative growth, a shift in priorities, strengthened relationships, and clarity in one's moral compass or life's purpose.

Organizational Patterns. Organizational patterns enable the family to move through life's transitional periods and daily challenges. Effective organizational processes are especially important when adversity strikes. Families that engage in flexible, creative approaches to problem-solving, adjustment, and adaptation are better able to move through the crisis. Also, when there is a sense of connectedness among families—a sense of mutual support and commitment—families are more confident in their ability to deal with adverse situations. Finally, having a connection to other family and community systems of support is vital to healthy family functioning, especially during times of stress. Resilience is uplifted by social and community connections and the ability to reach out to those supports when needed. Families that are connected to other social systems and know how to access them are more likely to successfully traverse the adverse event.

Communication/Problem Solving Processes. When families are faced with an adverse event, clear and honest communication is key. If details or information is left out of the discussion, family members are left to fill in the blanks which can lead to further distress. Honest discussions about a situation enable family members to make meaning of the event, make informed decisions, and select appropriate strategies for coping. Having a safe, empathic environment that allows for open expression enables family members to share how they feel about the challenge and where they are in the coping/healing process. Along these same lines, open communication fosters collaborative problem solving. Family members work together to set goals, evaluate previous strategies, find a solution, imagine a new way forward, and assign a collective meaning to the adverse event.

Military Readiness in Resilience

Readiness in the military defines personal and family readiness as "the state of being prepared to cope with the stressors of daily living and manage the competing demands of work life and personal and family life." (DoD Instruction 1342.22, 2012, p. 55). This readiness entails understanding and being able to navigate challenges of military life as well as having the necessary skills and access to available resources to effectively deal with these challenges. The DoD and service branches have developed guidelines and programs to enhance family readiness and resilience. The focus is two-pronged: service member resilience training and family resilience strengthening. For example, since 2009 the Army has conducted resilience training through their Master Resilience Training program. The Navy has two programs designed to enhance Sailors' resilience: Navy Warrior Toughness and Sailor Resiliency programs. The Air Force has a Department of Integrated Resilience website that contains a host of resources on a variety of topics geared toward building personal resources and resiliency (https://www.resilience.af.mil/). The focus of these programs is strengthening the military members. Family support organizations within each military branch also have family resilience programs that are specifically aimed at family readiness. This perspective views readiness as a state or condition of a person prior to experiencing stress. In contrast, Meadows et al. (2016) consider resilience the process or outcome of dealing with stressful events. Based on this, what role does the state of readiness play in complementing or enhancing the process of resilience?

Using the Families Overcoming Under Stress (FOCUS) program, Saltzman et al. (2016) examined how parental distress affected family members and family functioning. The findings confirmed that family processes that foster resilience can reduce distress and ineffective adaptation by military family members. These results support family resilience models that emphasize using preventive measures that foster and support healthy family resilience processes. Preventive programs such as FOCUS are aimed at strengthening resilience and thus military family readiness.

Assessment and Treatment Considerations

Building family resilience entails assessing family strengths instead of focusing on deficits and dysfunction. By involving the family in evaluating and exploring their own strengths, we build confidence, ownership, and agency within the family. This strengths-based perspective seeks to identify strengths while acknowledging the challenges and problems they face. Interviews play an integral role in the assessment process, building collaboration and exploring family members' perceptions of their strengths and abilities in resolving the situation at hand. Employing a strengths-based approach implies the practitioner holds similar beliefs as Walsh in that families have the capacity to overcome adversity and that they can emerge from the experience stronger and more confident in their ability to face future challenges. Similarly, Simon et al. (2005) identify four philosophical assumptions of practitioners who use solution-based treatments.

1. All families have the potential for growth and improvement at any time in their development and in any situation.
2. All families possess unique and specific forms of resilience, strengths, and resources that can be applied toward problem resolution and therapeutic goals.
3. Family resilience and resources often remain hidden or masked by the momentum and influence of the problem.

4. Families benefit from the practitioner's encouragement to recognize and apply their own resources toward solutions and growth (p. 432).

Simon et al. (2005) compared traditional (medical/psychological) vs strengths-based interventions. Comparisons include
- viewing the response to an adverse situation as dysfunction vs unsuccessful attempts to resolve the situation,
- the role of the clinician as expert vs collaborator,
- the nature of treatment having a problem-focus vs solution focus, and
- the desired outcome of decreasing family dysfunction vs increasing family resilience.

Strengths-based approaches have a positive and empowering effect on the therapeutic relationship, process, and outcome.

Treatment

The family resilience framework views the client-therapist relationship as a collaborative and empowering one. It is reciprocal in that everyone participates in identifying how a situation can be resolved, what resources are available, strengthening effective processes and developing new capabilities within the family unit. Walsh (2003) emphasizes "rather than rescuing so-called 'survivors' from 'dysfunctional families,' this approach engages distressed families with respect and compassion for their struggles, affirms their reparative potential, and seeks to bring out their best qualities" (p.14). One of the most significant take-aways from Walsh's work is that resilience is not a process of returning to a former state unharmed, but working through and surmounting the challenge, learning lessons along the way, and figuring out how to integrate the experience into one's life. There is an investment of work and an element of growth involved in this process. This idea, when communicated to family members, can help in their understanding of growth through adversity and lending meaning to their struggles.

Resilience and resiliency are an integral part of individual and family functioning. By focusing on programs and interventions that build and enhance these processes and traits, the Department of Defense and its service branches can bolster military readiness among its members and families.

Final Thoughts

Daily challenges of military life require members and families to be able to respond and adapt to change in healthy ways. The concept of resilience is vital to healthy family functioning and growth. Definitions and evolution of resiliency research grew out of stress theories and models:

- Research focus shifted from an individual to a systems perspective
- Resilience can be considered an outcome or a process
- Treatment evolved from problem/deficit orientation to family strengths and resources orientation

Caregivers can benefit from a clinician's application of the stress process model. Additionally, Walsh's development of the systems theory of family resilience forms the foundation for current resilience programs and interventions. Finally, the concept of resilience and its models form the basis for military family readiness training and intervention programs.

References

Blaisure, K. R., Saathoff-Wells, T., Pereira, A., Wadsworth, S. M., & Dombro, A. L. (2016). *Serving military families, 2nd ed.* Routledge.

Bush, K. R., Price, C. A., Price, S. J., & McKenny, P. C. (2017). Families coping with change: A conceptual overview. In C. A. Price, K. R. & Bush, S. J. Price (Eds.). *Families and change: Coping with stressful events and transitions* (pp. 3-23). Sage.

Boss, P. (2001). Definitions: A guide to family stress theory. In P. Boss (Ed.) *Family stress management* (2nd ed., pp. 39-70). Sage.

Department of Defense. (2021). *DoD Instruction 1342.22, Military family readiness.*

Hobfoll, S. E. (1989). Conservation of resources: A new attempt at conceptualizing stress. *American Psychologist, 44*(3), 513-524.

Hobfoll, S. E., Halbesleben, J., Neveu, J., & Westman, M. (2018). Conservation of resources in the organizational context: The reality of resources and their consequences. *Annual Review of Organizational Psychology and Organizational Behavior, 5*, 103-128.

MacDermid, S. M., Samper, R., Schwarz, R., Nashida, J., & Nyaronga, D. (2008). *Understanding and promoting resilience in military families.* Military Family Research Institute. https://www.mfri.purdue.edu/wp-content/uploads/2018/03/Understanding-and-Promoting-Resilience.pdf

Matthieu, M. M., & Swensen, A. B., (2013). The stress process model for supporting long-term family caregiving. In A. Rubin, E. L. Weiss, & J. E. Coll (Eds.). *Handbook of military social work* (pp. 409-426). John Wiley & Sons.

Meadows, S. O., Beckett, M. K., Bowling, K., Golinelli, D., Fisher, M. P., Martin, L. T., Meredith, L. S., & Osillia, K. C. (2016). Family resiliency in the military: Definitions, models, and policies. *RAND Health Quarterly, 5*(3), 12.

Pearlin, L. I., Menaghan, E. G., Lieberman, M. A., & Mullan, J. T. (1981). The stress process. *Journal of Health and Social Behavior, 22*(December), 337-356.

Pearlin, L. I., Mullan, J. T., Semple, S. J., & Skaff, M. M. (1990). Caregiving and the stress process: An overview of concepts and their measures. *Gerontologist, 30*(5), 583-594.

Saltzman, W. R., Lester, P., Milburn, N., Woodward, K., & Stein, J. (2016). Pathways of risk and resilience: Impact of a family resilience program on active-duty military parents. *Family Process, 55*(4), 633-646.

Selye, H. (1956). *The stress of life.* McGraw Hill.

Selye, H. (1983). The concept of stress: Past, present, and future. In C. L. Cooper (Ed.). *Stress research: Issues for the eighties (pp. 1-20).* John Wiley.

Simon, J. B., Murphy, J. J., & Smith, S. M. (2005). Understanding and fostering family resilience. *The Family Journal, 13.* 427-436.

van Breda, A. D. (2018). A critical review of resilience theory and its relevance for social work. *Social Work/Maatskaplike Werk, 54*(1). http://doi.org/10.15270/54-1-611.

Walsh, F. (2003). Family resilience: A framework for clinical practice. *Family Process, 42,* 1-18.

Walsh, F. (Ed.). (2012). *Normal family processes: Growing diversity and complexity,* 4th ed. Guilford Press.

The Emotional Cycle of Deployment
CHAPTER NINE

Deployments are an integral part of military life. When a service member deploys, it affects everyone—the service member, spouse, partner, and children. It requires logistical, emotional, and psychological preparation and adjustment by all family members (Dick et al., 2014). Chapter 4 covered deployments and their effect on the service member. In this chapter we look at how the entire family deals with deployments. In its simplest definition, a deployment is scheduled time away from home. The type of deployment dictates the length of absence and the level of risk or danger the service member may face. Deployments may be scheduled and routine, such as rotations on a ship or to a forward operating base. They may be unanticipated such as a response to national emergency. Regardless of the type of deployment, the various models suggest family members follow the same path of progression through the stages of deployment. These models and subsequent studies also suggest predictable activities and responses associated with each stage and offer coping strategies to minimize the negative outcomes families might experience. Common strategies throughout are preparation, communication, building/using support systems, and accepting that change is inevitable. In this chapter we look at the deployment process, family responses, and strategies and interventions to help family members move through the deployment process.

Types of Deployments

Deployments are scheduled time away from home unit and involve the movement of forces and equipment to specific areas. Depending on the nature of the deployment and branch of service, an entire unit or a select team may deploy. Sometimes service members deploy to fill unique positions as individual mobilization augmentees. This is a common role for some National Guard and Reserve members. The length of a deployment varies depending on the nature of the deployment and the branch of service. Deployments can last a few weeks or up to a year or more. Some military units have predictable deployment schedules which lend an element of stability and predictability for service members and their families. Other types can spring up and offer little notice to the military member and the family. There are websites that further describe the types of deployments and what family members can expect (e.g., militaryonesource.com) Types of deployments include training, natural disaster/humanitarian, peacekeeping, and combat.

Military readiness is essential, so oftentimes units conduct training exercises which may involve deploying to another location for training. Training may be a continuation or honing of existing skills or involve learning skills for a different environment. Additionally, these training missions may precede the deployment, extending the time away from home. A second type of deployment is for humanitarian purposes in response to natural disasters/emergencies such as wildfires, hurricanes, earthquakes, or volcanic eruptions. Finally, service members may deploy for peacekeeping and combat purposes. While all deployments have some element of risk or danger associated with them, a peacekeeping or combat deployment holds the greatest risk of injury or death.

The deployment cycle starts when a service member is notified of a deployment and flows through three basic stages: pre-deployment, deployment, and finally the return home or post-deployment. When a service member deploys, *all* family members find themselves facing a variety of challenges. We examine these within the context of the emotional cycle of deployment.

Emotional Cycle of Deployment

Several models of the emotional cycle of deployment exist (See Table 9.1); all primarily focusing on the family members left at home when the service member deploys: a simple 3-phase pre-deployment, deployment, post-deployment model; a 5-stage model by Pincus et al. (2008); and a 7-stage cycle presented by Logan (1987) and Moyses (2012). Although each family's response to deployment is different, there are commonalities as they adjust to the stages of deployment regardless of the frequency of them. The ability to cope with deployments in a healthy manner hinges on many enabling factors--strength of the marriage, preparation, communication, and "coping IQ"—having the resources (internal and social/community support) and resilience to handle separation and the inherent stressors of deployment.

Logan identified the stages of the Emotional Cycle of Deployment as experienced by Navy wives in the February 1987 US Naval Institute Proceedings journal. Although it was based on the experiences of Navy wives when their husbands deployed, it still has merit as evidenced by subsequent models based. Researchers have taken this framework and expanded it over the past 30+ years. Moyses at the Michigan State University Extension wrote a series of articles in 2012 about the effects of each stage on the military family. Other authors have added the service members' perspectives and responses as well. This chapter encapsulates various models of the emotional cycle of deployment, salient family responses and strategies to cope with the responses or minimize the stress associated with them.

Table 9.1

Emotional Cycle of Deployment Models

3-Stage Model	5-Stage Model Pincus (2008)	7-Stage Model (Logan, 1987; Moyses, 2012)
Pre-deployment	Pre-deployment	Anticipation of Loss/Departure
		Detachment and Withdrawal
Deployment	Deployment	Emotional Disorganization
	Sustainment	Recovery and Stabilization
	Re-deployment	Anticipation of Return
Post-deployment	Post-deployment	Return Adjustment and Renegotiation
		Reintegration and Stabilization

It's important to note that when we use the term cycle, we think of a starting point, flowing through various stages, then returning to the starting point. The National Military Family Association (2006) suggests using the term spiral of deployment rather than cycle when speaking of the deployment experience; there is no return to the original state. Family members learn from the deployment experience, grow, and use the lessons learned to navigate future deployments. People are not static entities. During the deployment process, all family members change and grow, so when the service member returns from deployment everyone experiences an adjustment period. While separation during deployment presents its own hardships, the post-deployment and reintegration phases tend to be just as challenging to navigate.

Pre-Deployment

The pre-deployment stage is typically defined as the time between notification of the deployment and the day the service member leaves. However, pre-deployment activities begin long before that as part of the military readiness posture. Early in a service member's career, there is a focus on planning and being

The Emotional Cycle of Deployment

prepared for both expected and unanticipated separations and deployments (Dick et al., 2014). This preparation involves logistical aspects of making sure personal, family, financial, and legal matters are in order and a remaining partner understands the deployment process. Notification of deployment sets off a flurry of activity and mixed emotions. The service member is focused on preparations for deployment while the partner/spouse is focused on a to-do list before departure. The service member is stretched between work-related activities and trying to get the home front prepared for the upcoming separation. Some of the legal and logistical activities include preparing/updating wills, powers of attorney, ID cards, health care for family members (especially for National Guard and Reserve families), and family care plans for single and dual-military parents. Legal considerations are especially important if the service member has a partner who is not a legal spouse or children who do not live in the home. Money is always an issue, so financial and budgeting plans need to be made to carry the family through the deployment. Additionally, service members may want to squeeze in visits with family and friends before departure. Threaded throughout this task-oriented phase are changing emotions that ripple through the household.

Tensions are high as family members deal with the news of the deployment. Anticipating the departure can elicit shock, denial, anger, fear, resentment, and guilt. Parents may argue about trivial things, they may become restless, irritable, or depressed. Children may also express anger and fear over their parent's deployment. The youngest children may not understand what is happening, but they can sense a change within the home. News of the deployment can trigger separation anxiety in both the spouse and children. Attachment theory can help explain the concept of loss, responses, and how to minimize or cope with separation during deployment.

Another aspect of pre-deployment is emotional detachment, a natural coping mechanism when anticipating loss. As the departure date draws near, partners as well as children begin to pull away from each other to buffer the pain of separation. Family members often shut down and stop sharing thoughts and feelings with each other. Their focus turns to the deployment stage and thinking about how they will manage the separation.

Deployment

The deployment stage begins as soon as the service member leaves and ends upon return. In the 7-stage models, the deployment is divided into three phases: emotional disorganization, recovery and stabilization, and anticipation of return. Pincus et al. (2005) include a sustainment stage which is similar to the recovery and stabilization stage. Dick et al. (2014) note that "deployment is a psychological, emotional, social, cognitive process that has both expected and unforeseen implications for the entire family system (p. 68). Service members and their families experience the deployment process with mixed emotions and reactions.

Service members are eager to do what they are trained to do, yet ambivalent, sometimes guilty about leaving the family behind. Going into unknown territory can be stressful, especially if it is their first deployment. Deployment conditions may be austere, cramped, and dangerous. The time away can create anxiety and worry, insecurity about the relationship, concern about the return home. It can also be a time to reflect on personal values and perspectives (Dick et al., 2014).

Family members also experience transition from known routines to taking on new roles and responsibilities. Partners and children may feel overwhelmed while others welcome the new independence and challenges. Children may struggle to understand their parent's absence and have difficulty with new responsibilities. Additionally, unforeseen circumstances may arise requiring the family to respond and adapt. The ability to cope and adapt to the new situation is the salient feature of the recovery and stabilization phase of deployment. Coping is dependent on the ability and willingness to seek out and use available resources. Support centers on military installations are designed specifically to address the needs of deployed family members by providing a variety of resources.

The Emotional Cycle of Deployment

There are three distinct phases to deployment: emotional disorganization, recovery and stabilization, and anticipation of return. The initial response to the service member leaving is emotional disorganization. It's a mixed bag of a) sense of relief that member has finally left, b) guilt, and c) feeling lost—without direction or purpose (Logan, 1987). There is a sense of disorganization navigating the unknown and figuring out a new routine. This can cause tension among family members. Sleeping and eating patterns are off; children may show signs of stress—regression, clinginess, struggles in school, mood changes, acting out, etc. After a while, the family settles in and move to the recovery and stabilization or sustainment stage.

The recovery and stabilization or sustainment stage is characterized by the family settling into a routine that works for them. As they become accustomed to the new routine, members gain self-confidence in their ability to handle situations and a sense of independence. This phase is also marked by establishing and using support systems (Logan, 1987; Pincus et al., 2005). On the other hand, the stress of managing family and household can lead to mental and physical health challenges for the partner/spouse. The separation, especially if marked by limited communication with the service member, can take its toll. The loneliness and increased responsibilities can result in infidelity, substance abuse, and child maltreatment. Additionally, if the marriage or relationship was rocky before the deployment, it may not survive the separation. The final phase of deployment—anticipation of return or redeployment—prepares the family for the service member's return.

The anticipation of return or redeployment phase is an emotionally and mentally busy time. This period is characterized by a burst of activity to get things ready in the home. Excitement and anxiousness are the overarching emotions. Family members are excited for the return, yet they are concerned about how they will all fit together again as a family. Everyone one has changed during the separation. What will the new family unit be like? This is also a time when partners/spouses begin to reevaluate their relationship. With newfound confidence and independence, spouses may be reluctant to relinquish some of their responsibilities. They begin to consider how to renegotiate roles and responsibilities once the service member returns. Overall, anticipating the reunion is a challenging time filled with unknowns and excitement.

Post Deployment

Post-deployment begins upon return to home station and family. Planning for post-deployment is important; however, the return home doesn't always cooperate with the plan. Delays happen and there are often work-related duties upon return such as securing equipment, debriefings, medical processing, etc. Post-deployment is filled with many conflicting emotions: anticipation, joy, fear, anxiousness, sadness, to name a few. For most coming home is a time of excitement because the service member is reunited with family and back on familiar territory. As the excitement of being back home subsides, the task of reintegrating into the family begins. Roles and responsibilities must be sorted out. Time does not stand still for either the deploying member or the family members at home. People change during deployments; those at home gain new skills and newfound independence. The deployed member may have undergone notable change as well. If the service member experienced physical injury or trauma, this is an extra source of concern and stress. The extent to which the service member needs care, the unpredictability of behavior due to PTSD, TBI, and depression, and the ability to continue serving in the military weigh heavily on the family.

The strength of the marriage prior to deployment influences the ability to reunite as a family and is a principal factor in successful reintegration. The separation can either further weaken the relationship or it could serve as an opportunity to reprioritize and refocus the relationship. Partners/spouses, experience the stress of deployment and extended absences. If there are no children in the family, partners may have less difficulty coping with the absence. On the other hand, having a family to care for helps pass the time. Often, partners can verbalize their feelings and seek out support when they are overwhelmed. In lieu of healthy outlets and support, some turn to substance abuse or infidelity as a source of comfort. Divorce may also happen when a spouse or partner cannot cope with deployment. Finally, the stress of deployments and long absences can affect parenting skills and jeopardize the health of children.

Additional Considerations for Children

There is no shortage of journal articles pertaining to the effects of deployment on children. What are some of the issues being explored in the research? Some studies focus on response to deployment based on the developmental stages of the child. Others examine whether there is a different reaction when a mother deploys vs a father. Those who developed the emotional cycle of deployment look at children's reactions during the stages of deployment. Additionally, boundary ambiguity and ambiguous loss are explored in the context of military deployments. These topics are easily found by conducting an internet search.

When a parent deploys, children may be left in the care of the other parent, grandparents, or relatives depending on the marital status of the service member. Military children respond to extended absences and reunification in a variety of ways depending on age, developmental stage, and the information and support provided by parents prior to the separation. Some of the salient reactions to separation include ambiguous loss, worry and anxiety about the parent's safety, and anger about the parent's absence and additional responsibilities they are asked to assume. A shift in routines also can cause anger and resentment. Young children may experience regression, sleep difficulties, and clinginess. Older children may experience troubles at school—academically and behaviorally. Adolescents may engage in risky behaviors or act out. Children of all ages may develop physical ailments and anxiety or depression as a result of stress and worry about their parent's absence. Finally, when a parent returns with issues such as a physical injury, PTS, or TBI, children can develop secondary traumatic stress response.

Regardless of age, children who struggle can benefit from mental health intervention to help them cope with the separation during deployment. On the other hand, there are many children who cope well with deployments and experience a strengthening of their coping ability and resilience. Cozza and Lerner (2013) note

> the severity of the stress, the proximity of the experience, the children's age and gender, their history of exposure to other traumatic experiences, their parents' or caregivers' functional capacity, and the availability of social supports all typically contribute to the outcome (p. 5).

Yellow Ribbon Reintegration Program for National Guard and Reserve Families

When National Guard and Reserve Forces return from deployment, the experience is much different than that of active duty members. Their military duty often is part-time, so they return to civilian life with civilian jobs, usually to a primarily civilian community. Military support systems that are available on military installations is absent. The Yellow Ribbon Reintegration Program (YRRP) was designed to address some of the disparities in services available to National Guard and Reserve Forces.

The YRRP was signed into law by President Bush as part of the Defense Authorization Act of 2008 to provide military members and families information and outreach services during the entire deployment cycle. The program has a three-pronged approach aimed at each phase of deployment. Efforts focus on military readiness of the service member, family, and the community during the pre-deployment phase through the creation and implementation of family education programs and counseling. Programs include financial and legal counseling, explanation of Tricare services, and the prevention of domestic violence. During the deployment, the YRRP provides activities to engage and support military families in caring for their physical, mental, and spiritual wellbeing. Online and in-person events are scheduled to connect families with each other. Stress management, legal assistance, and spouse employment programs are also offered. Finally, during the post-deployment phase the YRRP offers debriefings to connect the family with available services and help re-establish relationships with family, employers, and community. More information can be found at the Yellow Ribbon Reintegration Program website (https://www.yellowribbon.mil/) and in Harnett and Gafney's article "Ensuring Equity After the War for the National Guard and Reserve Forces: Revisiting the Yellow Ribbon Initiative" in Kelley, Howe-Barksdale, and Gitleson's book *Treating Young Veterans: Promoting Resiliency Through Practice and Advocacy.*

Navigating the Deployment Process

Successfully navigating the deployment process hinges on several enabling factors: preparation, communication, and coping IQ consisting of resilience of family members and use of support networks. Franklin (2013) notes that service members and families' response to deployment also depends on previous deployments and their attitude toward the military and this deployment. First, preparation is key to a healthy deployment experience by understanding the process and potential hurdles. Second, open lines of communication are vital during each of the deployment stages, but especially in the pre-deployment stage. How family members communicate during this stage sets the tone for the remainder of the deployment process. Third, identifying and building a support network helps build resilience and can ease the stressors of the deployment. As we found in Chapter 8, family resilience is a key component of military family readiness. Service branches offer programs designed to help families attain readiness. This readiness extends to having the necessary skills and access to available resources to effectively deal with deployments. When family members avail themselves of the family services offered on military installations, they improve their readiness to meet the challenges of the deployment process.

Each branch of service offers programs geared specifically toward deployments through their family support centers. Each branch uses a different name for their military and family support centers: Army Community Service

Centers, Marine and Family Programs, Navy Fleet and Family Support Centers, Military and Family Readiness Centers, and National Guard and Reserve Family Assistance Centers. Identifying and *using* support systems such as extended family members, friends, church groups and other community resources helps spouses and children feel supported and connected.

Preparation

Family readiness is an integral aspect of military life. The concept encompasses day-to-day military life skills and extends to the logistical and psychological preparation for deployment. Taking advantage of the services offered by family support centers helps build competency in coping with military life and strengthens family readiness. When the deployment notification comes, attending pre-deployment briefings and even counseling can help family members understand and better cope with deployment and separation. Many books and websites are geared toward helping military families prepare for deployments, some complete with checklists. Pavlicin's book, *Surviving Deployment: A Guide for Military Families*, was written in 2003, yet contains information that is still valuable today. Names of agencies have changed, but the checklists, advice, and considerations are pertinent. Just as important as pre-deployment planning is post-deployment planning. Homecoming can be an exciting and stressful time for all. It's important for partners/spouses to decide together what type of homecoming they would like. For many service members, a quiet reunion is preferred, especially if the deployment was dangerous or traumatic. Others are excited to have a big celebration. Communication is a large part of planning and often the key to successfully navigating the deployment process.

Communication

As mentioned in Chapter 8 Family Stress and Resilience, when families are faced with an adverse event such as a deployment, clear and honest communication is key. If details or information is left out of the discussion, family members are left to fill in the blanks which can lead to further distress. Honest discussions about the deployment allows family members to make meaning of the event, make informed decisions, and select appropriate strategies for coping. Having a safe, empathic environment that allows for open expression enables family members to share how they feel about the deployment. Along these same lines, open communication fosters collaborative problem solving. Family members work together to set goals, evaluate previous strategies, find a solution, imagine a new way forward, and assign a collective meaning to the adverse event.

Communication is vital in every stage of deployment. Sharing information about feelings and daily activities, seeking advice, and decision making can all be done with today's technology. Although some are reluctant to share the negative with their spouse, it is important to find a way to keep communication flowing. Establishing a communication schedule, if possible, also helps to allay concerns. Additionally, communicating with the schools and childcare providers about the deployment establishes a team approach to helping children cope with the separation. During the final phase, anticipation of return, communication with the service member and the family members is essential. It is important to talk about how everyone has changed during the deployment and how those changes may affect the reunion. Important milestones may have been missed, the children have grown, the adults have changed as well. Hopefully, these changes have been experienced and communicated throughout the deployment so there are no great surprises. Communicating with the children about the service member's return is important as well. Parents need to openly discuss the return with children and how they are feeling about the reunion. Children may not know or remember the parent; they may have mixed emotions about the deployment experience and the parent's return. It's important to sort those out prior to arrival if possible. Finally, post-deployment communication can be challenging; finding time to share all that has transpired during the deployment, an unwillingness or inability for the deployed member to share traumatic or difficult experiences, or simply needing time to reestablish relationships can hinder family communication. Conversely, effective communication and effective planning contribute to a strong coping IQ and healthy state of resilience.

Coping IQ—Resilience and Support Networks

Coping IQ consists of the resilience of family members and the availability and use of support networks. Each stage of deployment requires strategies to help family members cope. During pre-deployment, part of the preparation activities involve identifying available resources and shoring up or establishing a support network. These resources can be friends, extended family, church, schools, and family support centers. The deployment stage is the time for tapping into that support network and cache of resources. Franklin (2013) suggests parents find programs that will help them help their kids. Military bases often have programs designed for children whose parents are deployed. There are books and online programs specifically geared toward children of all ages. Parents can benefit from respite programs (free daycare) on base, as well as life skills and communication programs. Community organizations often cater to the needs of military families who have deployed members as well. Moyses (2012) suggests the following tips for coping with this stage: a) keep lines of communication open, b) maintain a familiar routine, c) include the service member in routine by talking about him/her, d) be patient, e) be positive and realistic about homecoming, f) involve the entire family in planning the homecoming, and g) seek help and support when needed. The final tip—seek help and support—is often employed as a crisis intervention rather than a preventive measure during deployments.

Building support systems and asking for help are key ingredients to successfully navigating the deployment process. Managing a family and household alone can be overwhelming. Spouses/partners often experience great stress, loneliness, depression, and anxiety if they are lacking a support network. Poor coping strategies such as overspending, substance abuse, infidelity, child neglect and abuse, can have profound consequences. Individual counseling and military programs offered by family support centers can assist

The Emotional Cycle of Deployment

parents who are struggling. These programs are both preventive and interventive in nature. While military mental health clinics are available to military members, there are Military Family Life Counselors at many family support centers. Tricare health system also covers mental health counseling. There are organizations and hotlines specifically for family members in need of guidance. There is the new 988 crisis line that family members can use. It is important for family members and mental health professionals to be aware of programs and services available to families with deployed members. Seeking assistance during the deployment process can ease the transition to the service members' return. Caplin and Lewis (2011) emphasize that social support is a key factor in service members' ability to effectively integrate back into the home and community in which they live. Support from family members, friends and community residents facilitates the process by offering validation and support to the service members' experience and sacrifices while deployed. Moreover, the homecoming service members receive vary tremendously and can have a profound effect on the service members' ability to navigate reintegration into the family, community, and secure any necessary services for their physical, mental, and spiritual well-being. When support services are scarce, veterans and families are on their own to deal with the fallout of deployment.

Military family members respond to military life, deployments, and separations in myriad ways. We have looked at some of the ways deployments affect families. It is important to note that many families cope with absences and deployment very well. For those who do not, a social worker may be called upon to assist the family. Understanding the deployment cycle and effects on the family helps the social worker employ appropriate and effective interventions. A family's ability to cope with deployments in a healthy manner hinges on many factors: preparation, communication, and coping IQ (having internal resources and a support network), and resilience to handle separation and the inherent stressors of deployment.

Final Thoughts

Deployments are an expected part of military life. Types of deployments include training, humanitarian/emergency, peacekeeping, and combat missions. The emotional cycle of deployment helps social workers and families understand the stages of deployment, salient responses to each, and strategies to successfully navigate through them. Successfully navigating through the deployment cycle includes factors of preparation, communication, and coping IQ (resilience and building and using support networks). Additional considerations are noted in this chapter for National Guard and Reserve families that may not have the same support programs/agencies that are found on military installations since they often do not live near a military installation.

References

Caplin, D. & Lewis, K. K. (2011). Coming home: Examining the homecoming experiences of young veterans. In D. C. Kelley, S. Howe-Barksdale, & D. Gitleson (Eds.), Treating young veterans: Promoting resiliency through practice and advocacy (pp. 101-124). Springer.

Dick, G. L., Kuntz, J., & Jennings, N. (2014). Deployment: When a parent goes to war. In G. L. Dick (Ed.) *Social work practice with veterans* (pp. 63-82). NASW Press.

Dick, G. L., & Marlow, D. (2014). Military Children. In G. L. Dick (Ed.) *Social work practice with veterans.* pp. 97-114. NASW Press.

Franklin, K. (2013). Cycle of deployment and family well-being. In A. Rubin, E. L. Weiss, & J. E. Coll (Eds.), *Handbook of military social work*, (pp. 313-333). John Wiley & Sons.

Harnett, C. and Gafney, M. (2011). Ensuring equity after the war for the national guard and reserve forces: Revisiting the yellow ribbon initiative. In D. C. Kelley, S. Howe-Barksdale, & D. Gitleson (Eds.), *Treating young veterans: Promoting resiliency through practice and advocacy* (pp. 175-217). Springer.

Logan, K. V. (1987). Emotional cycle of deployment. US Naval Institute. https://www.usni.org/magazines/proceedings/1987/february/emotional-cycle-deployment.

Moyses, K. (2012, July 23). *The emotional cycle of deployment: Stage one.* Michigan State University Extension. https://www.canr.msu.edu/news/the_emotional_cycle_of_deployment_stage_one_anticipation_of_departure

Moyses, K. (2012, September 12). *The emotional cycle of deployment: Stage three.* Michigan State University Extension. https://www.canr.msu.edu/news/the_emotional_cycle_of_deployment_stage_3_emotional_disorganization

Pavlicin, K. M. (2003). *Surviving Deployment: A guide for military families.* Elva Resa Publishing.

Pincus, S. H., House, R., Christenson, J., & Adler, L. E. (2001, Apr-Jun). The emotional cycle of deployment: A military family perspective. *Army Medical Journal.* https://stimson.contentdm.oclc.org/digital/collection/p15290coll3/id/898/

Community Capacity vis-à-vis Military, Veteran, and Family Support Programs
CHAPTER TEN

Military service as a single person is demanding. Caring for a family while serving creates even greater demands and challenges. Moreover, marriage and family integrity can be tough under typical circumstances; however, when you add to the mix extended mission- or training-related separations and deployments, stress can increase exponentially. In decades past, the military typically consisted of single men who joined or were drafted to serve in a war. Of course, there were military families, but often they were in the background and seen as a liability rather than an asset. Since the inception of the all-volunteer force, however, military families have grown to become an integral part of military society. Over several decades, the DoD and military branches of service have responded to the growing numbers of military families with increased housing, daycare centers, schools in remote or overseas areas, family resource centers, etc. As a young officer in the mid-50s, there was no such thing as base housing for my father and his growing family. Thirty years later when I served, many family resources on military installations existed, yet not as many nor robust as they are today. Having resources available to family members helps them navigate the winding and often stressful road of military life.

An abundance of programs mandated by the DoD and the Department of Veterans Affairs exist to help military members, veterans, and families deal with aspects of military life. Outside military installations, additional organizations and programs exist to help service members, veterans, and their

Community Capacity vis-à-vis Support Programs

families. The collaborative efforts of military, governmental, and community organizations build and sustain community capacity; a concept briefly explored in this chapter. We introduce the concept of community capacity and look at how military, government, and community agencies respond to the needs of military members and their families through programs and services offered both on and off the military installation.

Community Capacity

Community capacity is the ability of a community to support and sustain its members. Similar to the concept of military readiness, community capacity relates to what programs and services are needed to meet the needs of the community. Effective family functioning and coping often hinge on the broader community's support and ability to provide services to military families. Furthermore, building community capacity beyond the military installation helps strengthen individual and family resilience as well.

Community capacity involves the elements of shared responsibility and collective competence as well as formal and informal networks. Shared responsibility pertains to a concern for the general welfare of its citizens. When military family members sense that their community cares and is willing to support them, there is a sense of security that eases the stress of military life. Collective competence pertains to the ability to exploit resources and opportunities as well as fend off threats to community safety. When community organizations and individuals engage in collective competency practices and develop programs to support military family members, community capacity grows (Scott, et al., 2017). Heubner et al. (2009) note that "shared responsibility is a collective sentiment of concern, whereas collective competence is about taking action. In effect, community capacity is community readiness and performance in the context of opportunity, adversity, and positive challenges" (p. 219). Chaskin (1999) sums up community capacity this way:

> Community capacity is the interaction of human, organizational, and social capital existing within a given community that can be

leveraged to solve collective problems and improve or maintain the well-being of a given community. It may operate through informal social processes and/or organized efforts by individuals, organizations, and the networks of association among them and between them and the broader systems of which the community is a part (p. 4).

Community capacity within the military institution involves the coordination, collaboration, and complement of various formal and informal programs and initiatives. Formal programs are established by DoD and military department leaders and instituted by the various functions that are responsible for their operation on the military installation. Unit leaders also guide the development of programs that may be relevant to their units' unique mission, location, and circumstance. Finally, there are installation support organizations that often create programs and offer services to members and families. These can be both formal and informal networks that are formed through common interests and goals or through personal relationships and ties. These informal relationships serve an important function in identifying and sharing information on available services and resources. Huebner et al. (2009) emphasize the importance of informal networks when building and sustaining community capacity. Military members and families rely heavily on informal networks for information sharing and support; thus, formal support programs should contain an element of support and connection to informal networks. Extending community capacity beyond the military installation also helps strengthen military family resilience.

The greater community surrounding a military installation often has a variety of organizations whose goal is to provide some element of support to military members and families. They often fill in service gaps or supplement existing military programs. These can be military service organizations such as American Legion or Veterans of Foreign Wars. They may focus on helping those with service-related injuries such as Disabled American Veterans or Paralyzed Veterans of America. There are organizations that help wounded warriors and their families with customized homes or modifications and assistive devices such as the Gary Sinise Foundation. Other ways in which organizations join the support network and contribute to community capacity is through various programs or embedding helping professionals into their organizations. Schools can develop programs and hire social workers who are familiar with military issues to help military children succeed in school and cope with family stressors. Places of worship often create groups that are geared toward military members and families. Organizations like the YMCA and Big Brothers/Big Sisters partner with the local military installation to provide support services to military children and families. Finally, businesses sometimes create hiring practices that favor military family members or offer discounts on their products and services. All these different community agencies and organizations share in the goal of supporting the military family and its members.

Building community capacity--the ability to respond and support its members--is a main ingredient in the resilience of individuals and families. How well a military member/family can build and access a support network can mean the difference between effectively coping with military life and finding itself in a crisis situation. Moreover, healthy individual and family functioning relies heavily on the ability of the greater military community to coordinate and collaborate with myriad formal and informal support systems.

Military Programs for Service Members and Families

Military installations are self-contained communities, offering programs and services that you would find in a civilian community. Military members and families often live and work on military installations. There are houses, barracks/dormitories, commissaries (grocery stores), base/post exchanges (BX/PX/NEX/CGX; i.e., department stores), gas stations, Class VI stores (liquor stores), fitness and recreational facilities, health clinics, family readiness centers, chapels, libraries, daycare centers, and sometimes even schools located on military installations. The amount and extent of these services varies depending on the size, location, and service branch of the installation. For example, overseas installations typically have DoD schools on the installation for children yet may have limited on-base housing. National Guard installations often have limited services, such as a quick stop shop instead of a large exchange store or commissary and Coast Guard installations typically do not have on-base housing for their members. All these services focus on the general welfare of the military members who work there by supporting and enhancing the well-being of those military members and families.

Individual Support

Supporting individual military members runs the gamut of providing barracks/dormitory housing for single, lower ranking members or housing allowances to live in the community. There are dining facilities for those who reside in the barracks as well as restaurants for all who work and live on the installation. The fitness centers help members stay physically fit and typically have indoor and outdoor sports areas, weight and fitness machine rooms, and group exercise programs. Wellness centers assist in areas such as nutrition, weight and stress management, and help new military mothers return to fitness standards after the birth of their child. Personal trainers and massage therapists are often contracted to provide further assistance to military personnel. Activity centers such as officer and enlisted clubs, bowling alleys, skills development centers, and swimming pools are available for after work recreation, and unit gatherings. Medical clinics/hospitals, mental health services, and dental clinics focus on maintaining a healthy military force. Education centers help military members apply for their VA educational benefits and map out an academic path. Readiness centers offer a variety of programs to help new military members adjust to military life as well as help those leaving the military make the transition to civilian life. The chapels and chaplains tend to military members' spiritual needs, host social events, and provide counseling.

Community Capacity vis-à-vis Support Programs

Two other important programs that focus on the care of military members and their families are the Wounded Warrior Care and Intrepid Spirit Center. The DoD Warrior Care program (not to be confused with Wounded Warrior Project that you see advertised on television) focuses on helping ill or injured service members recover and reintegrate into their communities and providing caregiver support to family members. Each military branch has its own program: U.S. Army Recovery Care Program, US Navy Wounded Warrior, US Air Force Wounded Warrior, US Marine Core Wounded Warrior Regiment, and the U.S. Special Operation Command (SOCOM) Warrior Care Program (Care Coalition) for those members of special operations (https://warriorcare.dodlive.mil/Service-Programs/). Finally, the Intrepid Spirit Centers are funded by an organization called Intrepid Fallen Heroes Fund (https://www.fallenheroesfund.org/intrepid-spirit). The mission is to build centers on military installations that are dedicated to treating traumatic brain injury and post-traumatic stress for US and British military members. The goal of Intrepid Spirit Centers is to treat and mitigate symptoms thus enabling active duty service members to continue their careers. According to their website, 90% of those treated are able to stay on active duty. When military units take a holistic approach to the care and feeding of their members, individual readiness is enhanced.

DoD Military Family Readiness System

In the 1980s the DoD acknowledged that strong families lead to a strong military force. Responding to this acknowledgment, the DoD developed policies, services, programs, and resources that either specifically or generally mandate programs that support military families. The Military Family Readiness System is the framework from which and within which these policies and programs are developed and instituted (Le Menestrel & Kizer, 2019). These policies pave the way for establishing programs at military installations. Programs can be any service that strengthens family resiliency and enhances family functioning. Family readiness programs run the gamut of those focused on day-to-day living (life skills classes, budgeting, daycare, etc.), transition support (reassignment, retirement, separation from the military), deployment support services and youth programs. Short-term counseling and behavioral health support as well as family education are provided by military family life counselors. Furthermore, family violence/abuse intervention and prevention through the Family Advocacy Program and support services for family members with special medical or educational needs through the Exceptional Family Member Program are also provided on military installations. Finally, medical, mental health, and dental services are also provided to military members and families. Another important program is the Fisher House Foundation. The Fisher House Foundation builds group homes on military installations and VA campuses around the world providing housing, food, and transportation to families while their family member receives medical care at a military treatment facility. Eligibility for staying at a Fisher House is determined by the local installation commander. According to the website (www.fisherhouse.org) Fisher House Foundation provided housing and other services for 27,000 families in 2021.

Family readiness is the focal point of these programs. When families are supported by a strong network of services and resources, military members are better prepared mentally to successfully execute the mission. When members know their families will be taken care of, military members are more inclined to join or stay in the military. Voluntary and mandatory programs were instituted to support all members of the military family. Each military installation and branch of service has programs and services; for National Guard units and some Coast Guard units, they may be less visible and available. Offering these services to military members and families is part of building community capacity. Two important programs in the support and care of military members, veterans, and their families are the Tricare Health Management System and Veterans Administration.

Tricare Health Management System

Tricare is the health care program for uniformed service members, retirees, and their families. This program provides medical, dental, prescriptions, and specialized care for those enrolled in the program. Special care plans cover children with special needs, cancer care, WIC for overseas families, service members with battle injuries, and respite care for full-time caregivers. Tricare offers a variety of plans and the cost for enrolling in these plans varies according to a person's military status (service member, family member, or retiree). Since eligibility, plans and costs, and services tend to change, it's best to review the Tricare website for updated information. The various plans are described at www.tricare.mil/Plans/HealthPlans

Eligibility is outlined at www.tricare.mil/Plans/Eligibility

Special programs are listed at www.tricare.mil/Plans/SpecialPrograms

Dental plans are highlighted at https://www.tricare.mil/Plans/DentalPlans

Active duty personnel are seen at military clinics/hospitals. Retirees and family members may be seen as well when space and practitioners are available. Referrals are often made to off-base medical doctors/specialty clinics when these services are not available on base. Active duty members are seen at military dental clinics while all others are seen in the community. The various Tricare plans stipulate who is seen where and the extent to which family members may choose their care and practitioner. While many may find Tricare health management system confusing and tough to navigate, the advantage is the cost of military health care. The cost of enrollment and copays is minimal compared to civilian health plans.

Veterans Administration Programs

The US Department of Veteran Affairs is a comprehensive agency that provides a vast collection of services and programs to veterans and military members. Eligibility criteria are spelled out in Section 101 (2) of Title 38 of the US Code, Veteran Benefits, by defining a veteran as "as a person who served in the active military, naval, air, or space service, and who was discharged or released therefrom *under conditions other than dishonorable* [emphasis added]" (Title 38 US Code, p. 5). Those with service characterizations that are deemed dishonorable—other than honorable discharge, bad conduct discharge, dishonorable discharge, and dismissal (officer discharge)—are not eligible for VA benefits. Those who received Entry-level Separation (serving less than 180 days, usually while in basic training) also are not eligible for VA benefits.

The VA has eight priority groups/levels of care and access to services are based on the following criteria:
- Your military service history, and
- Your disability rating, and
- Your income level, and
- Whether or not you qualify for Medicaid, and
- Other benefits you may be receiving (like VA pension benefits)

You can read about the priority groups at this website: https://www.va.gov/health-care/eligibility/priority-groups

Priority groups 7 and 8 came to light when hearing about a veteran who was denied a COVID-19 vaccine because he did not meet the income requirement. Many veterans, family members, and those wanting to assist veterans may not realize that there are priority levels that require co-pays and that some priority levels are tied to income.

Another interesting bit of information is that veterans who previously served on active duty, then switched to service in the Guard or Reserves can apply for VA benefits. A person can still serve with a VA disability rating but can't receive both drill pay and disability payments. It's one or the other. The person must defer/suspend the VA disability payments until retirement or drill for almost no compensation.

The VA publishes a Federal Benefits booklet online. No longer available in hard copy, this 143-page online book outlines eligibility, benefits and programs that are available to veterans and their families. While most of the programs are geared toward veterans, three programs—VA backed housing loans, educational benefits, and transition assistance to include education and

Community Capacity vis-à-vis Support Programs

career counseling are extended to active duty personnel. These benefits are divided into five categories: health care, non-health care, education and training, special groups of veterans, and burial and memorial benefits. Health care benefits are extended to all veterans who meet the eligibility criteria. There are eight priority groups that stipulate care they may receive. Health care includes medical, mental health, dental, and specialty care, adaptive services and devices, pharmacy, referrals to outside clinics, long-term care, caregiver support, etc. Non-health care benefits include monthly compensation, aid and attendance stipends, compensation for clothing and transportation, and grants for housing or house modifications. Education and training benefits are available to both veterans and active duty members. Active duty members may use their Post 9/11 GI Bill or Montgomery GI Bill to pay for college or technical training at approved institutions. The Veteran Readiness and Employment (VR&E) program, also referred to as the Chapter 31, is available to veterans with a service-connected disability. There are also OJT and internship programs, campus advisory centers, and special employer incentive programs. There are also several supplemental educational grant programs such as the Yellow Ribbon G.I. Bill Education Enhancement Program. Assistance for special groups of veterans include housing, employment, health care and dental assistance for homeless veterans and their families; incarcerated veteran, the Veterans Justice Outreach, and reentry programs; and transition assistance and counseling programs for those leaving military service. Finally, there are burial and memorial benefits when the veteran and, in some cases, active duty member dies. Some of these benefits are tied to combat-related service. Burial benefits include being buried in a VA national cemetery and a headstone provided free of cost. There are many more programs offered by the VA which can be found at their website (va.gov) or in the benefits handbook (conduct an internet search for the VA Federal Benefits for Veterans, Dependents and Survivors for the most current edition).

For practitioners, the Department of Veteran Affairs website contains a tremendous amount of research articles, opportunities to sign up for monthly newsletters, and information about various veteran topics. The programs, services and resources provided by the DoD and VA for families and professional practitioners are another aspect in building community capacity to respond to the needs of the military. Beyond the military community, there are many other community programs that augment the Department of Defense and Veterans Administration's efforts to care for its military families.

Community Programs

Outside the gates are the greater communities in which military members, veterans, and families live and work. Veterans will often choose to remain near a military installation so their family members can finish school, or to avail themselves of the familiar services that military installations provide. Additionally, some veterans transition to a similar civil service job after their military career or seek employment with civilian contractors nearby. Still others seek completely different paths that have nothing to do with military life. Finally, there are those who struggle to find employment after military service due to their unique training or injuries sustained while serving. Community programs—government, private, or non-profit—often strive to fill the void to help service members, families, and veterans.

State and local governments often offer programs to assist in securing employment (job fairs, preferential hiring, etc.) and things such as free or reduced state park entrance fees, homestead (property tax) exemptions, disabled veteran license plates, etc. Additionally, many municipal and county courts have established Veteran Treatment Courts that focus on rehabilitation of military members/veterans who find themselves involved in the criminal justice system. College and universities may offer reduced tuition for service members and typically have a veterans' service center on campus to assist military members/veterans with various concerns regarding enrollment and successful participation in the academic environment. Military service related organizations such as the VFW or American Legion and officer and enlisted associations not only serve the military community, but they also work tirelessly to influence or enact government policy/legislation to support military members, veterans, and families. Religious centers focus on the physical and spiritual needs of military members/families through special programs, spiritual counsel, food banks, and housing/utility bill assistance. Finally, there are many local not-for-profit organizations that may be specifically designed to assist the military population or have a component of their program/services that focuses on the military. These may be focused on housing, employment, children's programs, respite care, family activities and programs, support groups for TBI or PTS, and health and wellness or alternative therapy programs such as music therapy, service dog training and pairing, or equine therapy.

Caring for and supporting the military community goes beyond the gates of the installation. It involves the commitment and wherewithal of local, state, and national leaders, organizations, and governments to foster individual, unit, and family resilience and readiness. The establishment and exploitation of this network of support systems at various levels is the essence of robust community capacity.

Final Thoughts

Successful military accomplishment relies heavily on how well individuals and families are supported during their military service by their community. Community capacity reflects the military and greater community's ability to adequately support military members and families. Military and government programs represent the formal systems designed to support and foster the mission; informal networks are the key to family members' awareness and willingness to use these programs. Community programs fill in gaps, work in concert with, and supplement government and military programs outside the gates of a military installation.

References

Chaskin, R. J. (1999) *Defining community capacity: A framework and implications from a comprehensive community initiative.* Paper prepared for the Urban Affairs Association Annual Meeting, Fort Worth, TX, April 22-25, 1998.

Defense Health Agency. (n.d.). *Warrior Care Recovery Coordination.* https://warriorcare.dodlive.mil

Fallen Heroes Fund. (n.d.). *Intrepid Spirit Center.* https://www.fallenheroesfund.org/intrepid-spirit

Fisher House Foundation. (n.d.). www.fisherhouse.org

Heubner, A. J., Mancini, J. A., Bowen, G. L., & Orthner, D. K. (April 2009). Shadowed by war: Building community capacity to support military families. *Family Relations, 59.* 216-228.

Le Menestrel S., & Kizer, K. W. (Eds). (2019, Jul 19). *National academies of sciences, engineering, and medicine; division of behavioral and social sciences and education; board on children, youth, and families; committee on the well-being of military families.* National Academies Press.

Scott, D. L., Whitworth, J. D., & Herzog, J. R. (2017). *Social work with military populations.* Pearson.

Tricare. (n.d.) Tricare Health Care Program. www.tricare.mil

About the Author

Susan Denise Barnes is a retired Air Force Chief Master Sergeant. She spent 25 years as an aircraft maintenance data systems analyst and held a variety of leadership roles throughout her career. Additionally, she served as program manager, curriculum developer, and instructor for enlisted professional development programs at several assignments. She holds a Master of Social Work degree and a Doctor of Education degree and has taught military social work courses since 2012. As a massage therapist, she focused on treating military members and veterans with post-traumatic stress and traumatic brain injury. This is her first book about social work practice with the military.

Made in the USA
Columbia, SC
03 March 2025